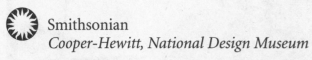
Smithsonian
Cooper-Hewitt, National Design Museum

NEW YORK

DESIGN FOR THE OTHER 90%

2

CONTENTS

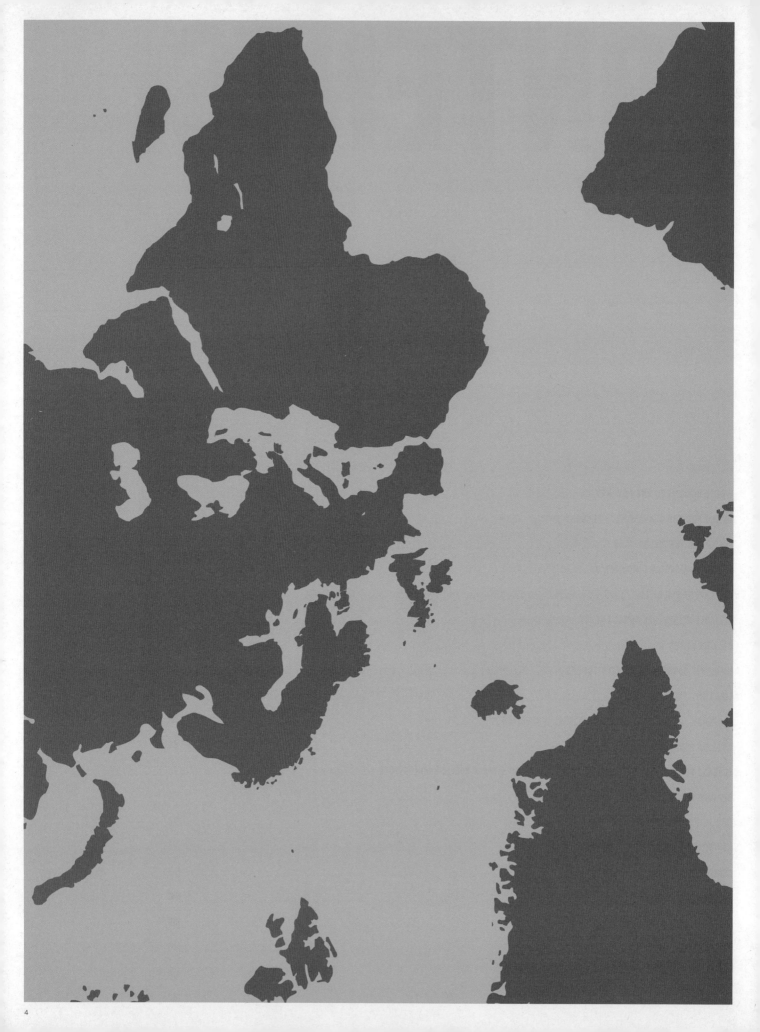

FOREWORD

BARBARA BLOEMINK

Where, after all, do universal human rights begin? In small places, closest to home—so close and so small that they cannot be seen on any map of the world. Yet they *are* the world of the individual person: the neighborhood he lives in; the school or college he attends; the factory, farm, or office where he works. Such are the places where every man, woman, and child seeks equal justice, equal opportunity, equal dignity without discrimination.
—Eleanor Roosevelt, remarks at the United Nations, March 27, 1953

Human beings have always used ingenuity to solve problems. Between 1960 and 1962, my family lived in Bogotá, Colombia, a beautiful city nestled in a plateau of the Andes Mountains. Colombia was, and is, a country where those with money and those without live adjacent to each other, rather than completely separated, physically and psychologically, as in most American and European cities. Our apartment was located on Carrera Primera, the uppermost street to the north, looking down at the wealthy parts of the city. On days when there was no school, our housekeeper would take me to visit her family, who lived up the mountain directly behind us. Climbing vertical paths, we visited her relatives' homes, largely built from purloined highway and road signs. Not only did these materials make the exteriors very colorful, but because of the signs' large size and heavy metal construction, the interiors were invariably waterproof, solid, and roomy. Illegally stripping an electrical wire off the public wiring poles enabled the residents to light their interiors and play radios. At the time,

1. Map of the world.

I was too young to be impressed by the creativity and resourcefulness of these recycled, remixed designs. Today, however, as I and all those I know spend our time searching for "design" as consumed by those who live "down the mountain," I wonder, Why has it taken so long for us to consider design as a word to be applied to the ingenuity of those living on the mountains behind?

The *Design for the Other 90%*[1] exhibition and book are intended to draw attention to a kind of design that is not particularly attractive, often limited in function, and extremely inexpensive. It also has the inherent ability to transform and, in some cases, actually save human lives. The works displayed and described have little relation to what we generally think of as design, and are rarely, if ever, illustrated in design magazines and journals, discussed at design conferences, or displayed in museum exhibitions. But we hope that exhibitions and books such as this one will gradually change this reality and help generate wider awareness and participation in this "other" kind of design.

In general, the word "design" is defined and based on how an object or concept balances three attributes: aesthetics, function, and cost. The "best" designs are usually equated with the highest costs, so that the designers' names attain an aura of privilege and distinction—and thereby bestow commensurate prestige on the user. Although the word design is visible everywhere—to describe the latest furniture, fashions, and accessories, or as the current panacea for generating consumer interest and increasing corporate bottom lines—objects such as those brought together for *Design for the Other* 90% are never visi-

2. Architecture for Humanity collage.

ble or discussed in our daily lives. Instead, we are surrounded by images of things designed for a culture with disposable income, capable of indulging in, and seeking fulfillment of, *desires* rather than genuine *needs*.

There is, however, another definition of design as intentional problem-solving, which best describes the methodology by which the many designers in this book work. Coming from all over the world, these men and women are "societal entrepreneurs" who use design to help alleviate the suffering of those lacking even the basic necessities. These designers recognize that by actively understanding the available resources, tools, desires, and immediate needs of their potential users—how they live and work—they can design simple, functional, and potentially open-source objects and systems that will enable the users to become empowered, self-supporting entrepreneurs in their own right.

In conceiving of this exhibition, one of the first challenges was how, with some sense of parity, to define the word "poverty," and thus be able to not only discuss farmers barely subsisting in Africa but also southern Americans who lost most or all of what they had in the devastation caused by Hurricane Katrina. Over time it became apparent that the issue was not how to wade through the hundreds of often competing statistics to properly define a term; but just as the designers in this book demonstrate, to look at how the potential users define what they need and want in order to feel empowered, self-reliant, and secure.

All humans share the same basic needs for clean water, shelter, food, transportation, medical aid, and access (fig. 2). Many of us are privileged and lucky enough to take them for granted, but for hundreds of millions of children and adults, they are barely or rarely attainable. Some of the designers' works are very basic and simple, yet they have astonishing effects. Half of the world's poor are suffering from waterborne diseases; and every day more than 6,000 children die from drinking unsafe water. As several of the designs described in this book attest, by changing disease-carrying water—whether filtered through colloidal silver applied onto ceramic pots (that have been used by more than 500,000 people), or via the LifeStraw personal mobile water-purification tool—into drinking water, countless human lives can be saved.

Other objects within the exhibition provide functions—the ability to see and read at night, to hear properly, to ride a bicycle even after losing a leg, to sit in church during Sunday services—that initially may not seem to be necessary for basic survival, but economically can raise the quality of users' lives and allow them to be sustained into the future (figs. 3, 4). With the globalization of the world, transportation and social participation have become increasingly vital aspects of life; at the same time, that information has become a highly valued international currency. Many today are concerned about the escalating division between those who able to easily obtain knowledge and information and those who are not. Global access has become a means by which individuals and cultures can learn from and be informed about the world. The lack of such access over time will result in increasing isolation, as well as the inability to

3. Jaipur foot and below-knee prosthesis. Designer/ manufacturer: Master Ram Chandra Sharma. Jaipur, India, 1968.

4. PermaNet®. Designer: Vestergaard Frandsen. Manufacturer: Vestergaard Frandsen S.A. Switzerland and Vietnam, 2000.

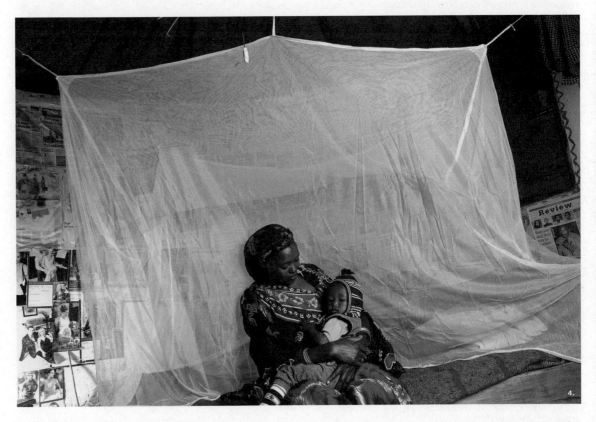

gain critical assistance and information in areas such as education, health, and medicine (fig. 5).

Many designers are devising ingenious ways to overcome issues of distance, power, and access. Firstmile Solutions launched the Internet Village Motoman for fifteen solar-powered village schools, telemedicine clinics, and the governor's office in Ratanakiri, a remote province of Cambodia (fig. 6). Meanwhile, through Operation Village Health's two monthly telemedicine clinics, patients in isolated areas of that country are given access to doctors at

Massachusetts General Hospital. A nurse from Phnom Penh makes a six-hour truck drive to each village to examine and digitally photograph the patients, and transmits the information by satellite to the doctors in Boston. To date, more than 600 clinical consultations have been conducted.

More than 200 international students and professionals collaborated with Design that Matters to develop the Kinkajou Microfilm Projector and Portable Library (fig. 7). Designed to improve adult literacy in rural West Africa, nearly 1,500 units, reaching 50,000 learners, are deployed in

5.

areas where up to seventy-five percent of the adult population is illiterate. The content of hundreds of books is stored on microfilm; and the projectors themselves use LED technology and run on three or four AA batteries. Many of the designs bundle multiple essential functions. The StarSight, for example, combines street lighting (which dramatically reduces crime rates at night) with solar-powered wireless networking and local network access. The system is intended to serve areas of rapidly growing urbanization in third-world countries.

This exhibition and accompanying book are intended to introduce the subject of designers actively designing for the "other ninety percent" of the world's population, rather than for traditionally wealthy consumers living largely in the industrialized world. They are also intended to applaud the works of those who are increasingly taking on these challenges, and perhaps to provoke additional designers to consider this end-user audience in their future designs.

The essays in this book represent a chorus of singular voices of designers who are using their creativity, experience, and knowledge to transform the means by which millions of people live. Above all, this book and exhibition pay tribute to the designers—whether professionals or self-trained, global or regional, students or professors, individuals or teams—who, rather than just adding another object or concept to our consumer culture, are looking around the world, identifying true problems and needs, and working with the users to design solutions to meet them.

The Lemelson Foundation, which supports invention and innovation to improve lives, has done much to expand this important field of design around the world. The Foundation has made possible both the *Design for the Other 90%* exhibition and the 2007 Summer Design Institute, a

program which trains teachers to use invention and design practices in the classroom. Significant support for the exhibition was also received from the New York State Council on the Arts, a State agency, the Esme Usdan Exhibition Endowment Fund, and the Ehrenkranz Fund. This catalogue is made possible in part by The Andrew W. Mellon Foundation.

As is always the case, the design of the exhibition and this book represent the work of many talented people who deserve our thanks. First I would like to offer sincere thanks to the exhibition curator, Cynthia Smith. Cynthia's personal commitment to humanitarian causes and her background as an industrial designer made her a perfect choice to organize, find, and negotiate all aspects of the final work. She did a superb job of locating the works for the exhibition, choosing and organizing the book authors, and putting her own stamp on the whole process. Thanks also to Cooper-Hewitt's team of Chul Kim, Head of Publications, Jocelyn Groom, Head of Exhibitions and Steven Langehough, Registrar, for their continuing commitment in terms of time and labor to the project; intern Andrea Lipps, who gathered the statistical information on the book's subjects; the Education department under the aegis of Caroline Payson; the fine Communications and Marketing team under the leadership of Jennifer Northrop; the Development team working with Caroline Baumann, Deputy Director, and Anne Shisler-Hughes, Director of Development; and all of the many other committed members of Cooper-Hewitt's staff whose efforts went into *Design for the Other 90%*. I'd like to also offer special thanks to the Museum's Director, Paul Warwick Thompson, and to the Board of Trustees for their continuing support, and to Esme Usdan, Kurt Andersen, and the members of the Exhibitions Committee for all of their kind and valuable assistance.

5. AMD Personal Internet Communicator. Designer: M3 Design. Manufacturer: Solectron and FIC. United States, Mexico, and Brazil, 2004.

6. Internet Village Motoman. Network: American Assistance for Cambodia, Operation Village Heath, Sihanouk Hospital Center of Hope, Massachusetts General Hospital, Harvard Medical School. Mobile access point and antenna. Designer/manufacturer: United Villages, Inc.; HyperLink Technologies, Inc. (antenna). United States, 2002–03. Solar Panel. Manufacturer: Kyocera Corporation. Japan, 2006. Ipstar broadband satellite system. Manufacturer: Shin Satellite PLC. Helmet. Manufacturer: S.Y.K. Autopart Import-Export Co., Ltd. Thailand. Motorcycle. Designer/manufacturer: Honda Motor Co., Ltd. Thailand, 2002.

7. Kinkajou Microfilm Projector + Portable Library. Designers: Design that Matters, Inc., in collaboration with students and professionals. Manufacturer: various contract manufacturers. United States, 2004.

6.

7.

WORLD DESIGNS TO END POVERTY

CYNTHIA E. SMITH

My world changed focus from the moment I watched the planes bring down the Twin Towers. I, like so many others, realized that our lives had changed. For the next two weeks, I roamed the streets of lower Manhattan looking for a way I could help in the aftermath; although I was trained as an industrial designer, I found nowhere my skills would be useful. As a result, I began questioning, *In what ways could I, as a designer, make a difference?*

TOWARD A MORE SOCIALLY RESPONSIBLE DESIGN

While a number of us from my architecture office volunteered with Imagine New York, a regional effort to get public input into the rebuilding of lower Manhattan, I knew there was more I could do. A political activist my whole adult life, I decided to run for office to try to make an impact locally. As my backup, I applied to school. I lost the race, but was accepted to the Kennedy School of Government. As a mid-career student at Harvard University I was studying with people from around the world with a wide range of professions, from diplomacy, law, and human rights to economic development, housing, and architecture. We all endeavored to help make the world a better place. After graduating, I felt I was armed with additional skills and ideas to make that happen. Arriving back in New York, I met Cooper-Hewitt's Curatorial Director at the time, Barbara Bloemink, who asked me to organize an exhibition about affordable designs to help people out of poverty. What I found as I began my research was a groundswell of work being done by a dedicated group of designers, engineers, architects, and entrepreneurs around the world to create sustainable solutions for improving people's lives. *Design for the Other* 90% highlights the many ways individuals and organizations are working to eliminate poverty and to give people around the globe a better standard of life.

A GROWING DESIGN MOVEMENT

A movement is growing both within the professional design community and the design, engineering, and architecture schools to direct our practices toward socially responsible, sustainable, humanitarian design. This represents a sea change, as the focus has shifted to underserved populations. In this paradigm, by working directly with the end users to determine what their needs are, designers are developing low-cost technologies which promote local economic growth and a way out of poverty (fig. 3).

Imagine you have only have $2 to live on for a day and have to choose among food, shelter, clean water, health, or pursuing an education. An instructor at the Massachusetts Institute of Technology, Amy Smith, asks her students to live on $2 per day for a full week to help them better understand the choices faced by almost half the world's population, 2.8 billion people, who can barely meet their own basic needs. One in six people around world, or 1.1 billion, barely exist on less than $1 a day, which is considered the level at which even basic needs cannot be met, and live with "poverty that kills." Amy Smith's MIT students supplement their $2-a-day immersion with living in communities in developing countries to better formulate designs that meet

1. Mad Housers Hut. Designer/ manufacturer: Mad Housers volunteers. United States, 1987.

the criteria for "appropriate technologies," which are simple, cheap, easy to produce and distribute, and meet a direct need.[2] Smith, a MacArthur Foundation fellow, develops her simple and efficient designs through D-Lab, a group which incubates in her classroom, develops in the field, and reports the high-impact results on a Web site.

In 2003, the United Nations designated Art Center College of Design in Pasadena, California, an official NGO, or non-governmental organization—the first design school to attain this status—to further Art Center's DesignMatters program for solving social challenges through design.[3] Similarly, Design that Matters, a nonprofit collaborative group out of MIT started in 2001, engages in "virtual design" of products and services for problems posed by international NGOs. Prototypes are researched and developed by volunteer engineers, designers, semi-retired professionals in collaboration with business, and engineering students. CITYbuild Consortium is bringing together over a dozen architecture schools with Tulane University to work directly with local community groups in New Orleans, Louisiana, for the reconstruction of that city's culture and buildings after Hurricane Katrina.[4] Harvard University's Kennedy School of Government and Business School joined together to find ways to work across sectors to solve social problems through social enterprise, beginning in the 1990s.[5] Stanford University now offers a class in entrepreneurial design for extreme affordability.[6] Other universities around the world, such as the University of Salford in England, conduct research in socially responsible design.[7] These are only a few examples of the many programs I came across in delving into this quickly emerging design area.

Dr. Paul Polak, a psychiatrist and founder of International Development Enterprises, calls it a "design revolution" that is applying design thinking to a new set of "clients." He is helping to teach a new generation of designers how to listen to rural farmers in the least developed countries to find low-cost products which will increase their agricultural output. IDE, an international nonprofit organization with programs in Bangladesh, Cambodia, Ethiopia, Myanmar, Niger, Nepal, Vietnam, Zambia, and Zimbabwe, employs market principles of income generation to help communities out of poverty.

Design for the Majority, a new interest group of the Industrial Designers Society of America, was recently formed by design professor Leslie Spear to help the more than five billion people who live on $10 or less a day. She believes we are in the middle of a "paradigm shift . . . in how design is currently being discussed and practiced, both nationally and internationally."[8] In 2005, the organization met to discuss emerging markets for the "Other Six Billion People," those underserved by current design services. Basing its conference on the UN Millennium Development Goals, the 2006 Aspen Design Summit called for the design community to partner with business, civic, and cultural sectors to end poverty in the developing world.

Several groups have emerged to serve as the connection and clearing house for different design disciplines to provide services to the underserved. The international group Engineers Without Borders links engineers with sustainable projects, from sanitation and energy to food production and water supply, to help people meet their most basic needs. Architecture for Humanity, which demands through its open competitions that architects "design like you give a damn," is flooded with submissions for its projects that address international humanitarian crises. Bryan Bell formed Design Corps, which partners with AmeriCorps to train young designers interested in social issues. Its participants work on projects for those who could never afford them, such as low-income rural communities and migrant farm workers. Several of these organizations informed and supported the selection of works for *Design for the Other 90%*, and have worked directly with some of the exhibition and book's contributors.

UN MILLENNIUM DEVELOPMENT GOALS
GOAL 1: Eradicate extreme poverty and hunger
GOAL 2: Achieve universal primary education
GOAL 3: Promote gender equality and empower women
GOAL 4: Reduce child mortality
GOAL 5: Improve maternal health
GOAL 6: Combat HIV/AIDS, malaria and other diseases
GOAL 7: Ensure environmental sustainability
GOAL 8: Develop a global partnership for development
For further information about the Millennium Development Goals, visit the UN's Web site: www.un.org/millenniumgoals

In 2000, the United Nations announced the Millennium Development Goals, a compact among wealthy countries to commit resources and among poorer nations to improve policies and governance, with a goal to cut extreme poverty in half by 2015. Momentum has been building: celebrities have made headlines bringing attention to the immense problem, and *Time* magazine displayed on its cover "The End of Poverty," Jeffrey D. Sachs's influential book. As Director of the UN Millennium Project, Sachs proposed investments and strategies in which high-income countries substantially increase international aid, to seventy cents for every $100 of national income (0.7% of GDP), for the least developed countries by 2015. Set in stages, the strategies

2. LifeStraw®. Designer: Vestergaard Frandsen. Manufacturer: Vestergaard Frandsen S.A. China and Switzerland, 2005 (current version).

focus on "rural productivity, urban productivity, health, education, gender equality, water and sanitation, environmental sustainability, science, technology, and innovation."[9] Others disagreed with this top-down approach and took an opposing stand. Former World Bank economist and author William Easterly thinks that "bottom-up searching—with lots of local involvement and feedback—will find the things that work to actually get results for poor people."[10] Several objects selected for *Design for the Other* 90%, such as improved anti-malaria bed netting, were developed expressly for mass distribution by international aid agencies; while others, like the micro-irrigation pumps, resulted from local involvement.

Some of this thinking has been around for decades. In 1973, an influential book of essays entitled *Small is Beautiful: Economics as if People Mattered* by British economist E. F. Schumacher identified what he termed "Buddhist economics." It called for production from local resources for local needs—the basic idea for appropriate technologies to which many of the designers in *Design for the Other* 90% adhere.[11] In 1971, Victor Papanek, a product designer for UN-ESCO, was one of the first advocates for socially responsible design in *Design for the Real World: Human Ecology and Social Change*, indicting not only the Western consumerist society but also designers, stating that "the genuine needs of man have often been neglected by the designer."[12] Traveling and living in the developing world, Papanek designed numerous low-cost products, including a radio made from discarded metal cans and powered by a candle for local production.

The projects featured in *Design for the Other* 90% were selected not just to highlight one philosophy or another, but also to open a discussion on the ways designers are looking for positive, sustainable results. Each of the selected objects opens a window into a unique story: an engineer in Nigeria creates a low-cost way to bring vegetables to market with a portable ceramic cooler; a group in Switzerland works with international aid organizations to stop the transmission of waterborne disease with a personal mobile water-purification tool (fig. 2); a multi-sector collaboration provides low-cost laptops directly to governments in an effort to increase literacy rates in the developing world. These solutions emphasize the variety of means by which designers from around the world have attacked the ongoing bane of global poverty. Some find unique ways to provide basic needs, while others address the root causes. Each does not stand alone, but is linked, building small footholds in often remote parts of the world which have begun to help improve the lives of individuals, families, and communities.

REVOLUTION CLOSER TO HOME

What initially started out as a project focused on designs for the developing world eventually expanded, as this was only one part of the story. Whenever I explained to others the concept behind *Design for the Other* 90%, I was asked if we were including works from the United States. Poverty exists in America; the World Bank describes this level as relative poverty, where household-income levels are a specific level below the national average.[13] One criterion for inclusion in the exhibition and book was that it needed to be a low-cost design intervention; it would also need to fit into our limited exhibition space. Such projects seemed hard to come by, but then we found the Mad Housers, an all-volunteer organization in Atlanta, Georgia, which builds "huts" for homeless people (fig. 1) from donated materials, providing a temporary shelter for those in need.

3.

3. Super MoneyMaker Pump. Designers: Robert Hyde, Martin Fisher, Mark Butcher, and Adblikadir Musa. Manufacturer: KickStart International. Kenya, Tanzania, and China, 1998.

book and exhibition, which directly relate to the meeting of basic survival needs such as clean water, these projects nonetheless affect and transform people's lives by providing an economic structure where they can learn skills, earn money, and become self-supporting over time.

When I looked across New Orleans's Lake Pontchartrain after seeing parish after parish filled with empty, boarded-up buildings, I began to understand the immensity of the hurricane's destruction. The lake was vast; standing on one side, you could not see the other shore, and all of that emptied into New Orleans. CITYBuild facilitates the connection between local community groups and architecture schools. This is not unlike the design taking place with the nonprofits in Asia and Africa, which work with rural farmers to determine what exactly they most need. I saw a number of design/build projects, "flagships" in the cultural and building reconstruction efforts in the Seventh and Ninth Wards, to include in the exhibition. A backyard museum (fig. 6) celebrating the Mardi Gras Indians was rebuilt for Ronald Lewis, founder of the House of Dance and Feathers, Mardi Gras Indian Council Chief, and member of the Northside Skull and Bone Gang, with the help of Patrick Rhodes, Project Locus, and architecture students from Kansas State University. Lewis's house was the first on his street to be rebuilt, and stands as an inspiration to others. An outdoor shade structure (fig. 5) was installed in a community garden so that the local Porch Cultural Organization could meet to discuss rebuilding efforts by another set of students, under the guidance of University of Kansas architecture professors Rob Corser and Nils Gore.

I traveled farther along the Gulf Coast to Biloxi, Mississippi, to meet with people who had come to help with the reconstruction and planning of this small city. Sharon Hanshaw started Coastal Women for Change to organize the women in her community to contribute a voice in what is being planned. While this was outside the scale of what we highlight in the exhibition, it does speak to how larger factors, such as economic development, help inform the design of a community. Many of the families who had small businesses hoped to return and rebuild despite overwhelming pressure to tear down areas and build more land-based casinos. Architecture for Humanity, in partnership with the Biloxi Relief, Recovery, and Revitalization Center, started a Model Home program which hosted a house fair for returning families and architects, who brought new house designs for selection. The designs present innovative solutions to the required higher elevations, some at twelve feet, and unique modified "shotgun" layout.

All of the people I interviewed and spoke with clearly wanted to stay and rebuild in New Orleans and along the Mississippi coast. The message they asked me to convey is that they continue to need help, as there is so much more work to be done.

Other projects came to our attention, including Public Architecture's Day Labor Stations, low-cost mobile centers to be built by the laborers themselves to accommodate meetings, classes, and sanitation facilities.

After Hurricane Katrina, Louisiana and Mississippi were the most visible signs in recent times of the income divide in this country. When I started to look for economic and cultural rebuilding projects along the Gulf Coast, I learned about two initiatives which grew out of the Aspen Design Summit, where Dr. Bloemink first met designers working in this field. I joined Sergio Palleroni of Katrina Furniture Project, and met Nik Hafermaas and Paul Hauge of Art Center's YouOrleans group (fig. 4) in New Orleans to see the rebuilding effort firsthand. Students, alumni, and professors from across the United States had gathered to explore how to help bring economic revival to the region through a branding campaign called YouOrleans, and to apply design skills to help a city still struggling to survive in the aftermath of a natural disaster. They were part of a larger story about other efforts along the coast. The Katrina Furniture Project, which is creating a cottage furniture-making industry from the debris left behind by the storm, was the brainchild of BaSiC Initiative's Sergio Palleroni. Joining with Green Project, a local reclamation group, Sergio and his students are making plans to employ and teach local residents to craft church pews for the ninety churches that were destroyed, stools and tables from beautiful two-hundred-year-old lumber found in the destroyed houses, and to help rebuild the local economy. While they differ from many other objects discussed in this

4. YouOrleans. Designers: Graphic Design department, Art Center College of Design alumni Jae Chae, Ayumi Ito, Atley Kasky; students John Emshwiller, Janet Ferrero, Matthew Potter; project director and department chair Nik Hafermaas; lead instructor Paul Hauge; in collaboration with the Designmatters initiative. United States, 2006–07.

5. Seventh Ward Shade Pavilion. Client: The Porch Community Center. Design/build team: University of Kansas School of Architecture. United States, 2006.

6. House of Dance & Feathers. Design/build team: Project Locus, Larry Bowne, Caitlin Heckathorn, and student volunteers from Kansas State University, Illinois Institute of Technology, and University of California, Berkeley. United States, 2006.

KATRINA FURNITURE PROJECT

RE

4.

5.

09/26/2006 6.

GLOBAL TECHNOLOGY RESPONDS TO POVERTY LOCALLY

Technological advancements are aiding the progress of a large range of work being done internationally to address developing countries' needs. The advent of the Internet and the availability of satellites and telecommunication hardware are making information more accessible, working in remote areas possible, and global collaboration feasible

Organizations like IDE are able to communicate with their various workshops and offices in India or Nepal, enabling them to work collaboratively and share information. Doctors in Boston can diagnose illnesses from remote rural clinics in Cambodia via "store and forward" technology. Cambodian "motomen" collect information via mobile

7. Ceramic Water Filters, Cambodia. Designers: Dr. Fernando Mazariegos, Ron Rivera, and IDE Cambodia. Manufacturer: Local private factory set up by IDE. Cambodia, 2006.

8. Big Boda load-carrying bicycle. Designer: WorldBike, Adam French (first phase design), Ed Lucero with Paul Freedman, Matt Snyder, Ross Evans, Moses Odhiambo and Jacob (second phase). Manufacturer: WorldBike and Moses Odhiambo's workshop. Kenya, 2002–05.

access points for uploading and international transmission. Architects in Europe or Asia can find out about projects after looking at Architecture for Humanity's Web site or receiving notice of it via email. I have been corresponding via email with designers in India, Nigeria, and South Africa about their development work and designs. Designers can now provide services to people who would not have received them before.

"Wiki"-technology Web sites have emerged to offer collaborative authoring, whereby visitors to the Web sites can add and edit content. In response to the natural disaster, the New Orleans Wiki was created for community groups and civic organizations to aid in the planning process in New Orleans. The site contains volunteer-maintained articles about the city, which allow groups to write proposals and plans. The neighborhood group has more input to the planning and design process as more information is available to the general public.

There are more and more ways for people living in remote areas to engage in income-generating activities and, through education, help the next generation out of poverty. Light-emitting diodes, or LEDs, the bright lights found in our pedestrian walk signals, illuminate low-cost lamps in Mexico so people can travel, study, or work longer and more safely. LED technology also illuminates projectors, enabling the education of women in remote areas about healthcare and adding a lightweight microfilm library to improve literacy in Africa and Asia. For the more than 1.6 billion people who lack a connection to electricity, solar panels which store the energy of the sun for later use enable them to live "off the grid," increasing their productivity and incomes.

Sometimes a design cannot be sustained because it is too expensive to make and the people who need it most cannot afford it. In South Africa, the Hendrikes brothers, one a civil engineer and the other an architect, devised an ingenious way to transport water by rolling it. Through trial and error, they developed a design that would last, but it cost too much for the end user. A great idea; but once they realized that the area's economic state could not support it, they ended their manufacture. They continue to look for alternate means to produce the product at an affordable cost. I have included an essay about this process in this catalogue, not to discourage those who might be considering how they can assist people living in poverty, but to show different approaches to problems and to encourage further exploration of sustainable solutions.

DESIGN MAKES A DIFFERENCE

So where did I find the international designers who are working to design for the ninety percent of the world who traditionally cannot afford "designed" work? I found them at universities and in small nonprofits, teaching people how to make inexpensive filters for clean water (fig. 7); designing bamboo treadle pumps for farmers to irrigate their crops in India; creating temporary shelters for earthquake victims in Pakistan; restoring the culture of a city like New Orleans; and creating ingenious ways to transport goods to market in Kenya (fig. 8). Many were suggested to me by those working in the field, others via seminars and conferences on humanitarian design. Far beyond any of the work discussed here, there are more and more designers working around the globe to provide access to water, food, shelter, education, health, transportation, and energy to people who

would otherwise have difficulty living their lives and supporting themselves. This exhibition and catalogue are not about providing expensive solutions. Instead, they are about low-cost, open-source designs that in most cases can be replicated and even sold by the users, thus providing them the means to become entrepreneurs in their own right. They provide an opportunity to tell the stories about a range of ways numerous groups and individuals are devising solutions to the causes of poverty.

Once an activist, always an activist. My hope is that this exhibition will open both designers' and the public's eyes to the numbers of people still living in deplorable conditions, and the multitude of ways any of us can take action. May these stories inspire young designers, established professionals, educators, journalists, and each of us to make a difference and help bring an end to poverty. For those who are not themselves designers but want to help, we have listed at the end of the book the Web sites of many of the organizations and designers discussed here.

DESIGN FOR THE OTHER NINETY PERCENT

PAUL POLAK

Ninety-five percent of the world's designers focus all of their efforts on developing products and services exclusively for the richest ten percent of the world's customers. Nothing less than a revolution in design is needed to reach the other ninety percent.

Transport engineers work hard to create elegant shapes for modern cars while the majority of people in the world can only dream about buying a used bicycle. As designers make products ever more stylish, efficient, and durable, their products' prices go up, but people with money are both able and willing to pay. In contrast, the poor in developing countries—who outnumber their rich counterparts by twenty to one—have only pennies to spend on hundreds of critical necessities. They are ready and willing to make any reasonable compromise in quality for the sake of affordability, but again and again, nothing is available in the marketplace that meets their needs.

The fact that the work of most modern designers has almost no impact on most of the people in the world is not lost on those entering the field. Bernard Amadei, an engineering professor at the University of Colorado in Boulder, tells me that engineering students all over the United States are flocking to take advantage of opportunities made available by organizations like Engineers Without Borders to work on problems such as designing and building affordable rural water-supply systems in poor countries. If students can make meaningful contributions in designing specifically for poor customers, why do designers continue to ignore this area? Is it because it is much more difficult than designing products for rich customers? Is it because they perceive that there is no money to be made? I do not agree.

HOW COMPLICATED IS IT TO DESIGN FOR THE POOR?

You do not need a degree in engineering or architecture to learn how to talk and listen to poor people as customers. I have been doing it for more than twenty years. The things they need are so simple and so obvious, it is relatively easy to come up with new income-generating products that they are happy to pay for. But they have to be affordable.

Twenty-three years ago, in Somalia, International Development Enterprises (IDE), the organization , I founded, undertook its first project by helping refugee blacksmiths build and sell 500 donkey carts to their fellow refugees. However, in Somalia, there are a lot of thorns in the dirt roads they traveled on, and nowhere a donkey-cart owner could buy tools to fix flat tires. So I went to Nairobi, Kenya, and bought tube patch kits and lug wrenches. I bought quite a number of good-quality, British-made wrenches that carried a virtual lifetime guarantee for $12 each, as well as a few $6 Chinese-made models that would be lucky to last six months. I offered both types of lug wrenches for sale to donkey-cart owners at cost plus transportation.

To my amazement, the Chinese lug wrenches sold like hotcakes while I failed to sell a single British model. How could this be? After talking to a lot of donkey-cart owners, I finally realized an operator could generate enough income in one month to buy ten British-made lug wrenches, but if

6. A micro-sprinkler in use on a small-plot farm in Nepal.

he did not have the money to buy a lug wrench today to fix a flat tire, he would earn nothing and might end up losing his donkey cart. So he bought the wrench he could afford today to stay in business and earn more money for tomorrow. I have heard the same story repeated over and over by the poor people I've talked to. For the 2.7 billion people in the world who earn less than $2 a day, affordability rules.

THE RUTHLESS PURSUIT OF AFFORDABILITY

Vince Lombardi, the famous coach of the Green Bay Packers, often said to his football players, "Winning isn't everything; it's the only thing." With one word change, the same sentiment applies to the process of designing products to serve poor customers: Affordability isn't everything; it's the only thing.

I have to confess that I am a born cheapskate, so the notion of putting affordability first comes naturally to me. When I need an umbrella, instead of buying a $38 designer model in the department store, I opt for a functional black one bought for $1 at the local Dollarama, where everything costs a dollar or less. I know the $38 model would last a lot longer, but I also know that I would probably forget it somewhere within a month. If that $1 umbrella keeps my head dry for just one rain shower or, better still, for a couple of months before I lose it, I've saved myself $37.

The rural poor think in much the same way, with one critical difference—they will keep that $1 umbrella in good working order for seven years, at the end of which it will have many patches on it and three or four improvised splints on the handle, yet still be usable. But there is another big difference. To earn a single dollar, an unskilled laborer in the United States only needs to work about ten minutes, while his counterpart in Bangladesh or Zimbabwe must work for two full days. To learn how to come up with affordable products for poor customers in developing countries, Western designers would do well to start with a brainstorming exercise to come up with a serviceable ten-cent umbrella.

HOW MANY ANTS DOES IT TAKE TO MAKE A HORSE?

Put yourself in the shoes of Peter Mukula, a poor farmer who lives along a dusty road twenty-five kilometers from Livingstone, in southern Zambia. If he could afford to buy a packhorse, he could make an extra $600 a year hauling vegetables to the Livingstone market. But there is no way he can beg for, borrow, or steal the $500 it would take to buy one. Can you think of a practical solution to Peter's dilemma?

Let me throw out a crazy idea: What if Peter could buy a quarter horse? Not a purebred quarter horse, but a horse that is a quarter the size of a regular packhorse. Let's assume that you could buy one of these miniature horses for $150 and that it could pack sixty kilograms. Would that work? Peter would earn less money each trip, but he could gradually use his profits to buy more miniature horses. Once he owned four of them, they would be hauling the same 240 kilos as a full-sized packhorse.

But even if a horse a quarter of the size of a packhorse were available, $150 is still far more than what he could afford out of his $300 yearly income. To make it affordable, Peter would need a miniature horse that is more like one-twelfth of a horse, which could carry twenty kilos and cost less than $50. Peter would probably have to carry another twenty kilos on his back to help make up the difference. After five years, he might be able to expand to a string of twelve pygmy horses. Only then could he earn the $600 a year that the packhorse he dreams of would provide.

Here is an even crazier idea: Suppose we could invent a way to harness the remarkable strength-to-weight ratio of the common forest ant. An engineering class in Germany designed tiny weights that could be attached to an ant's back and determined that forest ants can carry as much as thirty times their own weight. (A human can only carry about double.) How many ants would it take to carry the same load as a packhorse? An ant weighs about ten milligrams; if it can carry twenty times its weight, it can pack 200 milligrams. It would take one and a quarter million ants to carry Peter's 240 kilos. A million and a quarter ants would come pretty cheap, but designing the harness would be quite a challenge.

I have taken you through this imaginary design scenario to illustrate the central task of design for poor customers—coming up with breakthroughs in both miniaturization and affordability. The next step in the holy trinity of affordable design is to make the new product infinitely expandable.

FROM FOREST ANTS TO THE ASWAN DAM

If you think the process of breaking a horse into twelve af-fordable pieces is complicated, try wrapping your mind around the problem of breaking the Aswan Dam in Egypt down into millions of ant-sized pieces representing the small farms that could be nourished by the water stored in Lake Nasser. Big dams like Aswan are built to provide answers to the twin global problems of flooding and water scarcity. But when it comes to delivering irrigation water, extremely poor, one-acre farmers are usually left on the outside looking in.

THE NAWSA MAD SYSTEM

You may be wondering where the term Nawsa Mad comes from; it is Aswan Dam spelled backwards. It addresses perennial flooding and drought with exactly the same strategy used by the Aswan Dam, but shrunk down to one-four-millionth of its size so that it fits onto a two-acre farm and into a small farmer's pocketbook. Put another way, it is the ant to the Aswan Dam's horse.

Like most things in my life, I stumbled into the Nawsa Mad concept backwards. In May 2003, I was interviewing farmers in Maharastra, India, who were using low-cost drip systems to make the water in their open wells stretch a lot further than the flood irrigation they had been using.

But the sixty-foot-deep, twenty-five-foot-wide wells that were the only source of irrigation water during the dry season cost 100,000 rupees (about $2,000) to build. Because they were so expensive, only twenty-five to forty percent of the farmers in Maharastra owned a well. The rest earned a paltry income from rain-fed farming and survived by finding work outside the farm. However, rainwater ran off their fields in sheets during the summer monsoon season.

Could we find a cheap, simple way to trap some of this monsoon rainwater and store it to irrigate crops during the dry season, from March to May, when vegetable and fruit prices were at their peak? To create a miniaturized, on-farm version of the Aswan Dam, we had to find ways to: 1) collect monsoon rainwater on individual farms; 2) settle out the silt and mud in the water; 3) store it for nine months with no evaporation; 4) deliver it from storage to crops without wasting a drop; and, most important, 5) develop the whole system to be affordable enough for a poor farm family living on $300 a year, profitable enough to pay for itself in the first year, and infinitely expandable using the profits it generated.

Solutions for 1, 2, and 4 were easy. There are already all kinds of rainwater-harvesting systems in place that collect, settle, and store rainwater, and the low-cost drip-irrigation system designed by IDE could provide the means to deliver it efficiently to crops. The critical missing link was an enclosed, zero-evaporation water-storage system for individual farms that was cheap enough to pay for itself in the first growing season. We estimated that a farmer could reasonably be expected to clear $50 from drip-irrigated, high-value crops grown in the dry season using 10,000 liters of stored water. So we set a retail price target of $40 for the 10,000-liter enclosed storage tank. This was a daunting target since the cost of a 10,000-liter ferro-cement tank in India starts at $250. But we had already made progress toward finding an affordable solution.

People all over India were using open pits lined with plastic to store water for short periods. This was not a solution for us because most of the water would evaporate over six months in such a hot and dry climate. But the lined pits gave me the idea of placing a fatter version of an enclosed water bag into a pit. Jack Keller, an IDE Board member and internationally renowned water expert, closed the circle by pointing out that the optimal surface-to-volume ratio would be provided by a cylinder. So we came up with the idea of a ten-meter-long, double-walled plastic sausage in an earth trench (fig. 1). By using the earth for structural support, we reached our price objective of $40 for a 10,000-liter storage tank.

The fact is, of the 1.2 billion people in the world who earn less than $1 a day, some 900 million are small farmers who earn most of their living from what they can grow on their two-acre farms, split into four or five plots. Very few of them have access to irrigation water from big dams. Most of them live in climates with distinct monsoon and dry seasons, where affordable on-farm water storage and drip irrigation systems could enable them to produce income-generating, high-value crops in the dry season.

A $3 DRIP IRRIGATION SYSTEM

Almond growers in California invest millions of dollars in state-of-the-art drip-irrigation systems because they improve crop yield and quality as well as provide a miserly way to deliver water to the roots of plants. My colleagues and I at IDE have come up with something at the other end of the affordability scale—a kitchen garden drip kit that sells for $3 in India (fig. 2).

Larger low-cost drip systems now sell for $160 an acre in India—one-fifth the cost of conventional systems. The direct application of the building blocks of affordable design made this dramatic drop in price possible, and low-cost drip is rapidly establishing a massive new market for efficient, productive irrigation on small plots in India and other countries in Asia and Africa.

There is no need to maintain high pressure in the short plastic pipes that deliver water to quarter-acre plots. Cutting the pressure by eighty percent allowed us to cut the wall thickness of the pipes, thereby lowering the cost of material by eighty percent. The farmers themselves taught us how to make the walls even thinner and to provide a choice of wall thicknesses so they could pick a system that would last however long they wanted. We replaced expensive sand trap filters that prevent clogging with more simple and affordable filters, and we changed expensive high-tech emitters at drip points with simple plastic tubes that did not clog easily. We traded capital for labor by making drip lines moveable from one row of plants to the next. Finally, a farmer could start with a 20-square-meter system for $3 and expand it systematically to five acres by reinvesting his profits, highlighting the principles of affordability, miniaturization, and expandability I outlined earlier.

Mohan Nitin inherited his family's two-acre farm in Maharastra, an open well, and a five-horsepower diesel pump. But the well could only produce a quarter acre of flood-irrigated vegetables in the dry season, when prices are high. Mohan and his wife, his mother, and his two daughters, aged eight and eleven, were able to survive only by finding occasional work on neighboring farms.

Two weeks before my visit, Mohan's family invested $160 in an IDE Drip System for one and a quarter acres. This was only about one seventh of what he would have had to pay for a high-tech drip system of the same size; nevertheless, his mother had to sell family jewelry to pay for it. She beamed as she told me this because she now believes her family's poverty will end. Mohan and his family have planted sweet limes intercropped with eggplant as well as a variety of vegetables, and plan to add inter-cropped pomegranate. He believes he can earn more than $1,000 in the dry season alone, compared to the $150 or so he was earning before.

1. Trench-supported 10,000-liter water storage bag undergoing testing in India.

2. A $3 drip irrigation kit.

3. A drip-irrigated plot located outside Harare, Zimbabwe.

The dramatic drop in price for drip irrigation has now made it profitable for small farmers to start using drip on lower-value crops like cotton and sugarcane, and some of them are even irrigating alfalfa for their milk buffalos (fig. 3). I believe that low-cost drip systems like those developed by IDE will, over the next ten years, take over the majority of the world market for drip irrigation.

PEDALING TO PROSPERITY

This may sound like a large claim, but the enormous market potential for affordable technologies like IDE Drip has already been demonstrated in a powerful way. The proof lies in the phenomenal impact of the treadle pump, a simple, step-action pump that resembles a Stairmaster and can lift water from up to seven meters below ground (fig. 4). While IDE did not invent the treadle pump, we have reengineered it to be affordable for our rural, dollar-a-day customers. (On average, IDE's treadle pumps currently retail for about $40 in Asia and $90 in Africa.) Since IDE first began marketing treadle pumps in Bangladesh some twenty years ago, more than 1.23 million units have been purchased and installed

by small farmers at an unsubsidized, fair-market price. Using these pumps, many farmers have been able to double their net annual incomes, ensuring a better life and long-term prosperity for their families.

A $100 HOUSE

What dollar-a-day people in rural areas desperately need is a starter kit for a 200-square-foot house that they could borrow money on or sell if they had to, and which they could build for no more than $100. Homes in the United States and Europe are getting so expensive, it is becoming harder and harder for people to own one; remarkably, most of the 800 million or so people in the world who earn less than $1 a day and live in rural areas actually own the home they live in. But if they tried to sell it, they would get no money for it, and if they took it to a local banker as collateral for a loan, they would get nowhere. This is because many of these homes are made of sticks and wattle, with a thatched roof and dung floor, and have no value in the local market. Their owners have no opportunity to build something with real value at a price they can afford (fig. 5).

4. Bamboo treadle pump in use in Maharashtra State, India.

But in every village, there are a few families who have a house built out of brick or cement block and a tile roof, and these houses have both sales and collateral value. They accomplish this not by building it a little bit at a time, because that is all the money they have to spend, and construction loans simply are not available. I have seen far too many designs from Western architects for refugee shelters and rural dwellings that look elegant to the Western eye and start at $900, which is totally out of the refugees' and poor rural families' price range.

The no-value, stick-and-thatch home has a major flaw: it lacks a stable foundation and durable skeleton. All we need to start a salable, bankable 20-square-meter home is eight strong beams and a solid roof that does not leak. Initially, this durable structural skeleton can be filled in with local materials, for example, sticks covered with mud for the walls and thatch for the roof. Then, as there is money, the stick walls can be replaced with cement block or brick, twenty-five bricks at a time.

Access to affordable irrigation, seeds, ways to grow high-value crops, and profitable markets will speed up the home-building process. If, from the very beginning, the house is specifically designed to accept added modules, like a LEGO set, the family who lives in it can eventually own a house as big as they can afford. When the bankable house is completed, the family has a source of collateral so they can borrow money they need for inputs, implements, and livestock capable of increasing the income they earn from farming.

BUILDING MEMORIES

The fact that you do not need a degree in engineering or architecture to design life-changing products and services for poor people was amply demonstrated by Anne Willoughby, founder of Willoughby Design, a firm in Kansas City, Missouri, at the Aspen Design Summit in June 2006. "Your house is burning down," she said to the women in the audience after a two-day design studio for poor customers, "your family is safe, and you only have time to carry one thing out of your house. What would you save?"

The response from ninety percent of the audience was photo albums or other important family mementos. But most of the women in poor villages have no pictures of family members or of important events such as weddings and births. So she and two other Summit participants put their heads together and came up with the idea of creating a small army of village photo entrepreneurs. Women in villages would be given an opportunity to borrow funds to cover the costs of a starter camera, two memory chips, and a bicycle. They would go to neighboring villages, take family pictures, send a chip to town to be developed, and charge twenty cents a picture, or ten cents over their production cost.

Willoughby and her team had a vision of thousands of photo entrepreneurs making a living by providing family memories. They could also be trained to provide other important services, like seeds, drip kits, and training, so that poor women could grow profitable kitchen gardens in one region or provide health information and services in another.

THE PRINCIPLES OF DESIGNING CHEAP

My dream is to establish a platform for ten thousand of the world's best designers to come up with practical solutions to the real-life problems of the poor people of the world by following a few basic principles and practices. Miniaturization, the ruthless pursuit of affordability, and infinite expandability are the three building blocks necessary to design cheap. Now here is some music to go with the lyrics.

Thinking of poor people as customers, instead of recipients of charity, radically changes the design process. The process of affordable design starts by learning everything there is to learn about poor people as customers and what they are able and willing to pay for something that meets their needs. When in doubt, I resort to the "don't bother" trilogy:

· If you haven't had good conversations with your eyes open with at least twenty-five poor people before you start designing, don't bother.
· If what you design won't at least pay for itself in the first year, don't bother.
· If you don't think you can sell at least a million units at an unsubsidized price to poor customers after the design process is over, don't bother.

E. F. Schumacher was right on target by writing beautifully about smallness', even though he did not focus enough on affordability and marketability. A modern combine does not even have room to turn around on a typical quarter-acre plot of a small farmer, much less harvest it. Seventy-five percent of all farms in Bangladesh and India are smaller than five acres, and in China, half an acre. Since most of these small farms are further divided into several quarter-

acre plots, this is the gauge against which any new technology for small farmers must be evaluated.

For those trying to survive on a one-acre farm, a pinch of seed is much better than a bagful. For a long time, economists have talked about the "divisibility" of technology. You cannot take a tractor and cut it up into little pieces, so economists give it the rather curious but descriptive label of "lumpy input." [He needs to cite his sources for this.] But a twenty-kilo bag of carrot seeds can be easily divided into packets just the right size to plant two rows in a kitchen garden. Doing the same thing with mechanical technologies like irrigation, tilling, and harvesting devices is probably the most important challenge in designing cheap. A center-pivot sprinkler system is very efficient, costs a ton of money, and is designed to fit a 160-acre field. An Israeli drip-irrigation system (the first practical surface drip-irrigation system was developed in 1959 by Simcha Blass in Israel) is very efficient, costs a ton of money, and is designed to fit fields larger than five acres. How do we design a drip irrigation system that is just about as efficient as the Israeli system, costs less than $25, and fits perfectly into a quarter acre plot (fig. 6)? IDE has made great strides in solving these design problems, but there are thousands more like them that have yet to be addressed.

Affordability is the most important consideration in providing small farmers with access to income-generating technologies. Here are some guidelines I have created for designing cheap:

PUT TOOLS ON A RADICAL WEIGHT-LOSS DIET. You can cut the cost if you can find a way of cutting the weight. A good example of this is the one given earlier of the small drip-irrigation system where we cut the weight and the price of pipe by cutting system pressure by eighty percent. Doing this allowed us to also cut the wall thickness and weight of the plastic by eighty percent, with a corresponding drop in price.

MAKE REDUNDANCY REDUNDANT. Start out by asking potential customers how long they need the tool to last and how much they are willing to pay to make it last longer, and eliminate the redundancies that Western designers and engineers often take for granted.

MOVE FORWARD BY DESIGNING BACKWARD. Often, the most effective way of optimizing affordability is by going back through the history which leads to the modern form of the technology.

UPDATE THE OLD PACKAGE WITH CUTTING-EDGE MATERIALS. Revise outmoded designs with any new materials that may have become available, as long as affordability is not compromised.

MAKE IT INFINITELY EXPANDABLE. If a farmer can only afford a drip system that irrigates a sixteenth of an acre, design it so he can use the income it generates to seamlessly double or triple its size the next year.

Here are some basic steps that I have found can cut the price of almost any expensive technology by at least half:

· Analyze what the technology does.
· Set specific cost targets.
· Identify key contributors to cost for the existing product.
· Design around each of the key contributors to cost by finding acceptable tradeoffs.
· For the poor, the key affordability tradeoffs are: capital for labor, and quality for affordability.
· Make your changes based on field test experience.
· If you want to move your technology to a new area, adapt it through field tests.

THAT'S WHERE THE MONEY WILL BE

I keep asking why ninety percent of the world's designers work exclusively on products for the richest ten percent of the world's customers. Willie Sutton, the infamous bank robber, was once asked why he robbed banks. "Because that's where the money is," he replied. I suspect my question about the world's designers has exactly the same answer.

Don't get me wrong. I really have no problem with people who make money by designing products for the rich. Entrepreneurial brilliance deserves to be rewarded. What astonishes me is that a huge, unexploited market, which includes billions of poor customers, continues to be ignored by designers and the companies they work for. In

this, however, they are following a well-established tradition.

Today, you could ask the executives of Netafim, the world's biggest drip-irrigation company, why more than ninety-five percent of its products go to the richest five percent of the world's farmers, and they would probably reply, "Because that's where the money is." But think about this: If a hundred million small farmers in the world each bought a quarter-acre drip system for $50—a total investment on their part of $5 billion—it would amount to more than ten times the current annual global sales of drip-irrigation equipment. These millions of small farmers could put ten million additional hectares under drip irrigation and increase current global acreage under drip irrigation by a factor of five.

It is laudable that a small but growing group of designers is beginning to develop affordable products because they want to improve the lives of the world's poor. But there is only one truly sustainable engine for driving the process of designing cheap.

Because that's where the money *will be*.

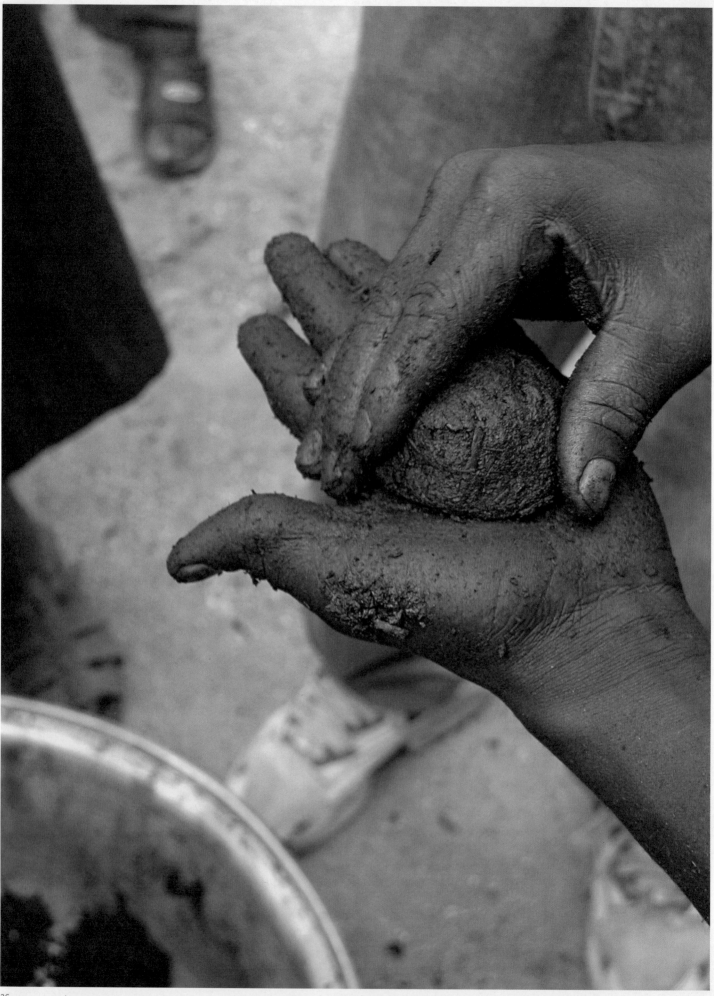

FUEL FROM THE
FIELDS

AMY SMITH

Nearly half of the world's population lives on less than $2 a day, and of these, almost 2.5 billion people use wood, charcoal, or dung for their cooking and heating needs. And while the total energy demands of the developing world are much smaller than in more industrialized regions, the dependence on these biofuels as an energy source has dramatic health, economic, and environmental consequences.

Throughout the world, more than fifty billion hours each year are spent collecting firewood. That is as if the entire workforce of the State of California worked full-time, forty hours a week, fifty weeks a year, doing nothing but collecting firewood. The economic impact of this is obvious, but it also affects education and gender equity. Children—a disproportionate percentage of them girls—are often charged with this task, and therefore have to miss school and the opportunities education can provide. As deforestation becomes more widespread, these effects will increase, as people will have to walk even longer distances to collect the wood to meet the energy needs of their families.

But even more striking are the health impacts of using wood, dung, and agricultural residues as a source of energy. The leading cause of death in children between the ages of one and five is not malnutrition, diarrhea, or malaria, but respiratory illness caused in large part by breathing the smoke from indoor cooking fires.[1] More than one million deaths each year are due to acute lower-respiratory infections, primarily caused by the small particles in the smoke of these fires. In the developing world, few people can afford clean burning fuels such as propane or kerosene, and they simply do not have access to electricity. Studies have shown that switching from dung and wood to charcoal as a cooking fuel would significantly delay at least thirty percent of these deaths.[2] But there is a severe environmental toll associated with using wood-based charcoal. Deforestation is already a critical issue in much of the developing world, and traditional practices of converting wood to charcoal wreak havoc on local ecosystems. As trees are cut down and burned *in situ*, the earth is sterilized by the heat and chemical residues, preventing regrowth and making the area even more susceptible to erosion. So while the health impacts of this conversion are compelling, the environmental costs may be too high.

The Fuel from the Fields project has developed a method for producing charcoal that does not have these negative environmental effects. Starting with agricultural waste materials and using simple, inexpensive equipment, it produces a clean-burning, environmentally friendly cooking fuel. The process and production methods are specifically designed at the grassroots level, so that the fuel is produced near the consumers, eliminating transportation issues. And since the process takes a waste material and converts it to a high-value product, there is a significant economic incentive and opportunity for microenterprise.

A small-scale farmer or entrepreneur can set up a charcoal-making business with an initial investment of less than $50. A 55-gallon oil drum can be modified to become the kiln for producing the charcoal (fig. 1). The drum is filled with the material to be carbonized—sugar-

5. Hand-forming briquettes was an earlier way of producing the charcoal, Fond des Blancs, Haiti.

cane residue, corncobs, millet stalks, or other agricultural waste materials—and then lit on fire. After several minutes, the drum is sealed to prevent oxygen from entering, and the material is allowed to carbonize. After a couple of hours, the process is complete and the drum can be opened. The carbonized material is then formed into briquettes using a binder made from cassava and a simple, hand-operated press. Cassava, also known as manioc, yucca, or tapioca, is a starchy root vegetable that is grown throughout the developing world, and when grated (fig. 2) and added to boiling water, forms a sticky porridge. The press, designed to produce high-density briquettes, can easily be made by local metal workers. The briquettes are left in the sun to dry (fig. 4), then are hardened by firing them in the kiln when another batch of charcoal is being made. Given the high value of charcoal in many areas, the entrepreneur can recoup the initial investment in less than three months and start earning a profit.

While the health and environmental benefits are compelling, it is the economics of the project that are most likely to drive its success. It is rare to find a project where there are no tradeoffs between the environment and the economics, or the economics and health. The Fuel from the Fields project is a win-win-win situation: the charcoal is clean-burning, so it has a positive health impact; it does not require that trees be cut down; and it provides income for the family, either by saving money that would otherwise be spent on charcoal or by producing excess that can be sold in the market.

This is probably the simplest technology that has come out of MIT in the last few years, perhaps even the last few decades, but it has the potential to have an immediate, significant impact on the lives of millions of people around the world. Right now, we are concentrating our efforts in Haiti, where over 5.2 million tons of wood are harvested for cooking fuel each year,[3] ninety-eight percent of the island is deforested, and many people spend more money on the fuel they use to cook a meal than on the food itself.

We originally became involved with the project when a group of students worked with a Peace Corps volunteer on improving the throughput of a device that made briquettes from waste paper. We became aware of the need for alternative cooking fuels, and the technologies that produce them, in Haiti. The students made several improvements to the briquette press, tripling its production. But unfortunately, these waste-paper briquettes did not burn as well as wood charcoal, and produced a lot of smoke. Thus began our quest to produce a briquette that burned as cleanly as wood-based charcoal but also used a waste product as a starting material.[4] We needed to develop a product that could compete with wood charcoal in the market as well as a process that would be effective in the local context.

We investigated what type of waste was available in the village, and found that there was a plentiful supply of *bagasse*, crushed sugar-cane stalks left over after the juice has been removed. We also realized that it would be necessary to turn the bagasse into charcoal in order to make a cooking fuel that did not produce a lot of smoke as it

2. Grating the binder ingredient cassava, a starchy root vegetable, Fond des Blancs, Haiti.

3. Making the binder, Jukwa market, Ghana.

4. Briquettes dry in the sun, Fond des Blancs, Haiti..

burned. Our first task then was to find a simple, inexpensive way to carbonize the bagasse and form it into briquettes.

The first few months were spent at MIT developing this technique. We decided to use a 55-gallon drum as the kiln, as they are widely available in the developing world and can be modified easily to increase the airflow needed to burn the bagasse at a high enough temperature to produce good charcoal. Next, the stalks of carbonized material had to be crushed and formed into briquettes. For this we needed a material to bind the charcoal fragments together. One of my students, from Ghana, knew of a dish called *konkonte*, a very sticky porridge (fig. 3) made from cassava. Even small amounts of konkonte were effective at holding the charcoal together, and we were able to form briquettes by hand (fig. 5). We were ready to test the process, but were unable to do so at MIT, since there was no ready supply of bagasse in Cambridge, Massachusetts.

Political instability prevented us from returning to

Haiti right away, but after a year or so, things settled down and we were able to go to the village of Petit Anse to perfect the process. The timing of the burn is critical: if it burns for too short a time, the bagasse does not fully carbonize; if it is left for too long, it burns away. Within a few days, we worked out these details. We trained our first class in the Ekol Chabon ("Charcoal School") and brought samples of the briquettes back to MIT for testing. We ran experiments comparing the sugarcane charcoal briquettes to wood charcoal, and found that, although our charcoal was comparable in terms of its smoke production, it only burned for about half as long. In addition, the briquettes crumbled and fell apart as they burned, leaving a portion of the charcoal unburned. We needed to find a way to produce briquettes that held together better and could burn for as long as wood charcoal.

Back in the laboratory, we started doing experiments on how to make high-density briquettes, and soon developed a hand-operated device which formed briquettes that burned as long as the wood charcoal (figs. 5, 7). A couple of design iterations doubled the output of the device, reduced its cost, and improved its manufacturability. But while they did not crumble when burning, these briquettes were susceptible to being crushed during transportation. A serendipitous discovery led us to a method for hardening the briquettes.

Unable to sun-dry the briquettes in the rainy New England spring, we simulated the sun-drying process by baking them in an oven at a low temperature. We found this was not only an effective way to dry the briquettes, but these briquettes were also much harder than those that had dried in the sun. Further investigation showed that drying temperatures of greater than 300 degrees Fahrenheit significantly increased the toughness of the briquettes. The question now was, How do we use this information to produce a more durable briquette without requiring any extra equipment or input of energy?

We knew that there must be a way to use the heat of the burning bagasse itself to fire and harden the briquettes. We tried placing the briquettes on top of the kiln after it was sealed, but once the kiln was covered, it cooled off too quickly to harden the briquettes. Then we tried putting the briquettes around the outside of the drum while it was burning, but here the temperatures were too hot, and the briquettes burned away. Finally, we tried placing the briquettes inside the kiln itself, just before sealing the drum, having faith that once the drum was covered, the oxygen-free environment inside the drum would prevent the briquettes from burning up. And indeed, this method worked, producing a briquette that was tough enough to transport to the market to sell. We were now ready to introduce our method to a wider audience.

We started doing demonstrations of the technique at a variety of sites around the world to get feedback from farmers and villagers. Our community partners in Haiti developed several improvements we incorporated into the process. And in Ghana, we made further modifications and experimented with carbonizing other types of waste materials. One of the most promising discoveries was making charcoal from corncobs (fig. 6), which remained intact during the carbonization process, and thus were ready to burn immediately after being removed from the kiln. This simplified the process considerably, eliminating the need for the binder and press. It also reduced the initial investment required to start making charcoal to just $10. A farmer could start earning a profit from his or her charcoal business in less than a week.

We have now begun to disseminate the charcoal project in Haiti, and hope to establish a countrywide program over the next few years. We have trained nearly a hundred people in the manufacturing techniques, and will continue to work with them to get their feedback and share lessons learned as we move forward.

The charcoal project is just one of several technologies that we are working on in D-Lab (the D stands for development, design, and dissemination): We are developing technologies which help communities monitor and maintain the quality of their water resources and help small farmers add value to their crops. We are creating lab equipment to expand the capabilities of rural health clinics and field laboratories. We are also training a new generation of designers, better equipped to design for the other ninety percent.

One thing I feel is especially important in designing for developing countries is that the designers should have a good understanding of the context in which they are designing and of the people using their products. Although I am not currently working on projects there, my Peace Corps experience in Botswana—especially my training program in the village of Molepolole—critically shaped my understanding of these issues. It was there that I learned to carry water on my head, and noticed how heavy the bucket was; and I learned to pound sorghum into flour and felt the ache in my back. I woke up at five o'clock in the morning to get wood to light the fire to boil the water for the morning meal. I learned these things from Tebalo, the woman who ran the household in which I lived; I also learned from her the many demands on the average African woman and the incredible strength with which she faces them. I stayed with Tebalo for a month, eventually learning to carry water without spilling half of it on the journey home, to grind grain without knocking the mortar over and losing it in the sand, and to light a fire quickly and efficiently to start heating the water for the day. And I came to understand, as a designer, the importance of technologies that can transport water or grind grain. I knew how far I needed to walk to gather the wood for the fire and appreciated the effects of deforestation and the need for alternative fuels.

When I teach my class about international development, I try to pass on this knowledge, but more important, I try to give the students experiences so that they too will become empathetic designers. For one assignment, students live on $2 a day for a week so that they can begin to understand the tradeoffs that must be made when their resources are limited. After they complete the first semester, the students have an opportunity to travel to a developing country and work with a community partner in the field. It is my hope that while they are there, they too will spend some time with a bucket of water on their heads and a grinding pestle in their hands. In addition, I have the opportunity to change the way they think about engineering and design—to recognize the complexity and the constraints of the developing world as a legitimate engineering challenge. And I have a chance to share something of my philosophy of design.

There have been three revolutions in design for developing countries that have influenced my approach. In retrospect, they all seem like common sense, but each in its turn was a significantly new approach to how products were de-

signed for people in these regions. The first of these was
the appropriate technology movement, based on the work
of E. F. Schumacher in the early 1970s. In his book, *Small Is
Beautiful*, he was one of the first people to rethink the context and scale of technology for development. He stressed
the need for technologies that create jobs which use locally
available materials and match the human resources necessary for the technology to function. The second revolution
is that of participatory development. Technologies were
developed that were appropriate to their surroundings, but
they reflected what the designer felt were the issues or
problems of a community, rather than reflecting the views

of the community itself. Participatory development in-
volves the members of a community in identifying the issues they face as well as the resources they have to address
them. In this way, developments are more responsive to
the real needs of the community and better maintained
once they are installed. The third, current revolution is the
notion of co-creation, of teaching the skills necessary to
create the solution, rather than simply providing the solution. By making the technology transparent to the users
and by involving the community throughout the design
process, the users are ultimately equipped to innovate and
contribute to the evolution of the product. Furthermore,
they acquire the skills needed to create solutions to a much
wider variety of problems. This leads to greater empowerment of the community, often in surprising ways.

Reflecting back on the charcoal project, what struck
me most was the passionate reaction of the people in the
training seminar. Deforestation is an issue that concerns
many Haitians, and it is with great frustration and sorrow
that they recognize how limited the viable cooking -fuel
options are in much of the country. The infrastructure and
resources are not in place to provide them with practical
alternatives. This simple technology changes that. They
now know how they, as individuals, can help prevent
deforestation. By gaining this knowledge, they have
acquired the skills they need to change their world.

DESIGN
TO KICKSTART INCOMES

MARTIN FISHER

As an engineer, I am convinced that technology has a critical role to play in ending the scourge of global poverty. Finding and developing such technologies have been my life's work for more than twenty years, and in particular since 1991, when I teamed up with Nick Moon to establish KickStart. The tools and technologies our organization has designed have already helped more than 230,000 people in Africa escape from poverty, but we have only scratched the surface of what is needed and what is possible. It has been an exciting journey, with both failures and successes, and a lot of learning.

I started on this path in 1985, after finishing my Ph.D. in Mechanical Engineering at Stanford. I was uninspired by my prospects for employment—teaching at a university or conducting research for the military or big oil companies—so I went to Peru to hike in the Andes and ponder my future. It was there that I first encountered extreme poverty, and began to think about how every civilization in history had advanced through technology and invention. I returned from Peru determined to use my engineering skills to help the poor, and received a Fulbright fellowship to go to Kenya to study the Appropriate Technology Movement.

The Appropriate Technology Movement was inspired in the mid-1970s by E. F. Schumacher's book *Small Is Beautiful*. According to Schumacher, small-scale, locally made technologies in the hands of the poor would help bring an end to poverty, and this concept had quickly become all the rage in development circles. However, by the time I arrived in Africa in 1985, I discovered that the Appropriate Technology Movement had been declared dead. Once again, development agencies had spent millions of dollars with very little lasting impact.

I expected to be in Kenya for ten months; I stayed for seventeen years. I spent the first years studying what had gone wrong with the Appropriate Technology Movement and worked with a major nonprofit agency to implement "integrated rural-development programs." This had become the new fashion, and it involved providing a large amount of development resources to a small geographical area in the hopes that this would raise people out of poverty. We used state-of-the-art methods, but when we went back to the communities a few years later, we found that our work had few enduring effects. The community water systems we had built were crumbling. The income-generating groups we had trained had collapsed, and the things we had given away had created dependency rather than empowerment. Disappointed, I tried to find out what had gone wrong and how we could fix it, and also why forty years and trillions of dollars in development projects had actually left Africa deeper in poverty. During this period I met and worked closely with Nick. The lessons we learned during this time—and those we continue to learn—formed the foundation on which KickStart was built.

One of most important lessons was that the poorest people in the world are also among the most entrepreneurial—they have to be just to survive. They do not want handouts; they want opportunities. Nick and I created KickStart to address this fundamental fact.

1. Samuel Gicharu, a farmer from Kaharati of the Maragua District in Central Kenya, sells his French beans for export.

2. A farmer on his Super MoneyMaker pump, outside of Nairobi, Kenya.

3. Compacting the blocks with the MoneyMaker Block Press in Jinja, Uganda.

4. Teresia Mukoshi of Nairobi, Kenya, cooking yellow beans on her Kenya Ceramic Jiko Stove.

I hope that *Design for the Other 90%* will inspire others to address social issues through design and innovation. And to this end I would like to share a few of the most important lessons that we have learned about how to use technology to help abate poverty.

FIRST THINGS FIRST: INCOME

If I could offer one piece of advice, it would be this: What poor people need most is a way to make money. Today, everyone in the world lives in a cash economy, and we need money to feed our families, buy clothes, build our houses, pay for healthcare, and educate our children. Even in the poorest parts of Africa, a subsistence lifestyle is no longer viable, and without a way to make money, people simply cannot survive. Too often, designers for the developing world fail to understand this most basic fact,

and focus instead on trying to make life a bit easier for the poor. But in order to have a significant impact on ending poverty, we need to focus on developing innovations that can be used directly by the poor to generate new income (fig. 2). In other words, the devices have to be used to produce goods or services that can be sold on the local market. In this way, whoever owns the device can use it to make money. This is KickStart's fundamental principle.

THE POOR DO NOT GENERALLY LACK TIME AND LABOR

It is tempting to design devices for the poor that will save them time and labor—after all, we pay dearly for such devices. However, time and labor are two things that many poor people have in abundance. Unless they have a way to make money with the saved time or labor, they are unlikely to invest much in such devices. For example, as long as they can get water from a free source, very few poor families will dig a well on their plot (which will cost them money) just to get drinking water—even if that source is many miles away. They make a decision that the time saved getting drinking water is not worth the initial costs of digging the well. For them, this money is better spent on basic food, clothing, shelter, healthcare, and education.

MONEY-SAVING DEVICES ONLY MAKE SENSE IF THEY ARE CHEAP

Some devices are promoted to help users save money. But the very poor live hand-to-mouth, and spend almost every penny as soon as they earn it. They have little money to save and even less to spend on money-saving devices. In Africa, the poorest people buy cooking oil and spices by the teaspoon and kales by the leaf. Cash flow is their biggest constraint, and, unless there is a way to offer them credit, it is difficult to get them to invest in a product that will save them money.

There are a few exceptions to this rule, and they are instructive to study. The Kenya Ceramic Jiko (KCJ) is a fuel-efficient charcoal cooking stove first designed in the early 1980s (fig. 4). It is forty percent more efficient than a common charcoal stove, and costs only about $2 more. Users of the KCJ save money because they need less charcoal, and at the same time the demand for charcoal—one of the biggest causes of deforestation—is reduced. The KCJ required millions of donor dollars to be spent on promotion over a fifteen-year period before it finally took off, but it now commands seventy percent of market share.

To an inventor who is working on an idea that will save poor people money, I offer this guideline: The product needs to sell for not much more than the price of a chicken in the local marketplace. A chicken is a luxury that even the very poor can afford from time to time. If the cost is this low, and the cost savings created are significant, you may have a successful product. If the cost is much higher (as it is for example with solar electric lanterns), then, unless financing can be provided, the only buyers will be the emerging middle class who already have enough money to cover their basic needs.

NOT INCOME OVER TIME, INCOME NOW

A new tool or technology for the poor must generate significant income in a very short period of time. So if an investment takes a long time to pay for itself, or goes bad altogether, they will go hungry for many months. Because the vast majority of the world's poor are rural farmers, we have to think in "farm time." Farmers are used to putting their money in the ground (in the form of seeds and fertilizer) and waiting three to six months to recoup their investment. This is another of the guiding design principles we use. Our tools have to completely pay for themselves in less than six months—preferably closer to three months.

UNDERSTAND THE POOR AND SOLVE THEIR PROBLEMS

In designing for the world's poor, there is too often a focus on developing things that "we" think "they" need. We design technologies that address a problem we have defined, without understanding the true needs of the people we are trying to help. Solar cookers are a good example. There are many clever designs for cookers which allow users to harness the power of the sun to prepare meals. The idea is that these cookers save forests from being cut down, slow global warming, and reduce the time required to collect firewood. These are laudable goals, but in most places, poor families prepare their largest meals in the evening, when the day's work is done. They prefer to cook inside so their neighbors cannot see what they are cooking, and often rely on a cooking fire for warmth, light, and to help repel mosquitoes. Moreover, poor families are unlikely to buy solar cookers unless they are very cheap and there is absolutely no other locally available cooking fuel.

THE POWER OF IRRIGATION

KickStart started by developing the means to make low-cost building materials, such as building blocks, out of soil and cement (fig. 3). Then we developed a technology to extract cooking oil from sunflower seeds. By 1997, we realized that to increase our impact we needed to focus on solutions for the eighty percent of Africa's poor who are small-scale farmers. They eke out an existence on small plots of land—often less than an acre per family. Their biggest asset is their land and their strongest skill is basic farming. We needed to help them leverage these assets, and irrigation was the missing piece. With irrigation, a farmer can grow crops all year round, instead of only once or twice a year when the rain comes. They can grow high-value crops such as fruits and vegetables, and, best of all, they can bring them to market in the dry season, when no one else has crops and the prices are high (fig. 1). But poor farmers in Africa cannot afford petrol pumps for irrigation, and almost none of them have electricity. So we developed a line of low-cost, manually operated irrigation pumps, appropriately named MoneyMaker Pumps. These lightweight, portable pumps can pull water from wells as deep as twenty feet or from rivers and ponds, and push it through a hose pipe under pressure to efficiently irrigate crops (fig. 6).

AVOID GIVEAWAYS—CREATE DIGNITY, NOT DEPENDENCE

From the very start, we at KickStart have sold our products. We do not give our pumps away, and this has caused some controversy, but we remain firm in this for a few reasons.

First, we want to create a sustainable solution to poverty, and no giveaway program can be sustainable. By selling our pumps, we create a sustainable supply chain. Every party has a vested interest in making our pumps, spares, and accessories available to anyone who wants one.

Second, we want to be as cost-effective as possible—moving as many people out of poverty for the least amount of money. When people buy something, they value it and are more likely to use it. These early adopters are more driven, more entrepreneurial, and more likely to succeed. Their success helps to inspire their more cautious neighbors and relatives. With giveaways, there are more likely to be a lot of early failures, and the technologies may never take off.

A great technology without a supply chain and promotion will have no impact. Perhaps the biggest reason that the Appropriate Technology Movement failed was because it tried to use a supply chain which ignored some of the basic rules of economics. It relied on the romantic notion that a new tool or technology could be made by individual end users or by local artisans spread across the countryside. The idea was that this would be more sustainable, create local jobs, and provide the valuable new technology. The idea was appealing, but fundamentally flawed. You and I are not asked to build our own automobiles, computers,

5. Felix Muiruri with his MoneyMaker Hip Pump on his farm in Maragua District, Kenya.

lawn mowers, and cell phones. They are made in large quantities in big factories. The economy of scale created by centralized manufacturing lowers the price, making the product affordable and ensuring higher quality and reliability. KickStart does the same thing. By centralizing our manufacturing in the most advanced factories available, we can produce high-quality, durable products at a lower cost (figs. 7, 8). Wholesalers and middlemen move these goods from factory to marketplace, making a profit in the process. A network of more than 500 local retail shops in three countries stock and sell our pumps. This supply chain needs no artificial support, and will exist as long as there is consumer demand. KickStart also uses donor funds to market the new technologies and generate demand. As with any new product, this takes both time and money. When you are selling an expensive item to the poorest people in the world, it takes even longer and is more expensive (again, the KCJ is a perfect example). But eventually, we will reach a point where we can end our marketing efforts and sell each pump at a profit, which we will then reinvest in developing new technology and expanding into new countries. This is a sustainable supply chain.

Third, there is a question of fairness. I have heard people say that it is not "fair" to ask poor people to invest in their own future, but is it fair to give one person or one village a gift when there are others just as needy? By making our products available through the marketplace, they are available to everyone, without patronage or favoritism. This is perhaps the hardest lesson for someone who wants to do good in the world. We see people in desperate need and want to alleviate their suffering. This spirit of generosity is human nature at its best. But as noble as this motivation is in the giving, it is demoralizing in the receiving. When people invest in themselves and their own futures, they have full ownership of their success, and that creates dignity.

INDIVIDUAL OWNERSHIP WORKS BEST

A good question to ask about any program is, Who will own the new technology? If the answer is unclear, or vague, then the program is unlikely to succeed in the long term. We have learned that individual ownership works better than group ownership. Africa is covered with failed community-owned technologies—tractors, water pumps, ambulances, water purification and irrigation systems, et cetera. The list goes on.

There is a common idea that poor people will come together for their collective benefit, or that "investing" in a community is more cost-effective or efficient than working with individuals. There are some situations where this works, like building roads or farmers' cooperatives. But it is much less likely to be effective with the joint ownership of a physical asset. The problem is that if everybody owns an asset, in reality, nobody owns it, and if nobody owns it, nobody will maintain it. Unless there is a way to extract a payment from everyone who uses the asset to cover the costs of maintenance, repair, and replacement, you have the classic free-rider problem.

It comes down to this: The poorest people in the world are just like you and me. No matter how community-minded we are, we will take care of the needs of our family first. And we value the most the items we had to work for.

DESIGN FOR AFFORDABILITY

Our best-selling Super MoneyMaker Pump can be used to irrigate more than two acres of land, and on average the users make $1,000 profit from selling fruits and vegetables in the first year of use. We continue to work to reduce the cost, but at $95, it is still too expensive for many families.

In response, we designed the Hip Pump, which can irrigate almost an acre and retails for less than $35. It looks like a bicycle-tire pump pivoted on a hinge at the end of a small platform. However, unlike a bicycle pump, it uses the operator's whole body. It is lightweight, portable, and extremely easy to use.

The Hip Pump has been a tremendous success: its initial production run of 750 units sold out almost immediately. One of them was bought by Felix Mururi, a young man from rural Kenya. He had a wife and three children to support, but they owned no land. Felix left his family to seek work in Nairobi, where he managed to earn $40 a month working in a restaurant in the city's slums, sending what he could home to his wife and children. When he saw the Hip Pump, he realized he could make more money farming back in his village. He saved his money, bought a pump, went home, and rented six small plots of land. He grew tomatoes, kale, baby corn, and French beans, which he sold to middlemen who took them to the city. Felix planted different crops on each of his small plots so he would have harvests at different times of the year. When we visited Felix three months after he started using his pump, he had already made $580 profit, and he and his wife were talking eagerly about buying land and building their own house. This small pump had enabled Felix to turn his own sweat and drive into cash, look after his family, and plan for his future (fig. 5).

MEASURE THE IMPACT OF WHAT YOU DO

Measuring real impact or outcome is where many would-be social entrepreneurs fail. The number of products you have sold or distributed tells the world nothing. You have to measure the change you are hoping to create with your invention. It is hard and expensive to do, but it is vital. We have learned a great deal from our impact-monitoring efforts. Not only does it enable us to measure ourselves against the goals we have set, it has also been hugely valuable in the design and improvement of our products and marketing efforts.

These are KickStart's core values, and they come together to create a very cost-effective and sustainable way to help people help themselves out of poverty. None of these principles are unique to KickStart or our technologies.

6. A farmer waters her French bean crop with water from a MoneyMaker pump, outside of Nairobi, Kenya.

7, 8. Kenya Vehicle Manufacturers (KVM), located in Thika, north of Nairobi, is one of the companies KickStart partners with to manufacture MoneyMaker Pumps.

They can be applied to many other technologies to make a real difference in the world. Each of these is important individually, but in our experience it is their combination that makes them truly effective.

Finally, for those people who are driven to innovate for the developing world (and also for those who are eager to fund such efforts), I offer this test. A truly successful program to develop and promote new technologies and/or business models needs to meet the following four criteria:

DOES THE PROGRAM CREATE MEASURABLE AND PROVEN IMPACT?

This means that you need to carefully define the problem you are trying to solve, then carefully monitor and measure the actual impact you are having on that problem. In the case of KickStart, we are trying to bring people out of poverty by enabling them to earn more money. So we carefully measure how much more money the buyers of our technologies make as a result of owning them. If a program cannot create and prove real impact, then it is not worth implementing.

IS THE PROGRAM COST-EFFECTIVE?

There are limited funds for developing and promoting new technologies, and we need to ensure that whatever is done uses these funds efficiently. "Cost-effective" is a subjective measure, so we offer this comparison: KickStart spends about $250 of donor funds to take an average family out of poverty, whereas a more traditional aid program claims on its Web site to do the same for $2,750.

IS THERE A SUSTAINABLE EXIT STRATEGY?

One has to ensure that the benefits will continue to accrue for both the existing and new beneficiaries, even after the donor funds are depleted. Creating a program that continues to depend on donor funds forever is not a viable solution. There are four different ways that an effort can become sustainable: 1) build and leave in place a profitable supply chain to continue providing the goods/services; 2) hand over the program to a government which will fund it using tax money; 3) create a local situation that can continue to prosper without the injection of any new outside funds, for instance, establishing a local group savings and loan (merry-go-round) system; 4) completely eliminate the problem, such as eradicating a disease.

IS THE MODEL REPLICABLE AND SCALABLE?

The problems we are trying to solve—poverty and climate change, among others—are very large in scale, and it is expensive to develop new technologies and new business models. So we want to ensure that the technologies themselves as well as the dissemination models are not too dependent on specific local conditions, and can be easily adapted to many different settings and locations.

Incorporating all of these guidelines into your work will be a challenge, but great inventors and designers enjoy a challenge. I can tell you that this experience has been an exciting, sometimes frustrating, often exhausting, and immensely satisfying journey. I wish you a fantastic journey of your own.

7.

8.

KICKSTART'S DESIGN PRINCIPLES:
Any tool or technology KickStart produces must meet all of the following design criteria:

INCOME-GENERATING—Any tool must have a profitable business model attached to it.

RETURN ON INVESTMENT—The business opportunity must be available to thousands of people, and the business must be profitable enough that the entrepreneur recoups his or her investment in six months or less.

AFFORDABILITY—We design our tools to retail at less than a few hundred dollars, ideally less than $100.

ENERGY-EFFICIENCY—All of our tools are human-powered, so they must be extremely efficient in converting human power into mechanical power.

ERGONOMICS AND SAFETY—Our products must be able to be used for long periods of time without injury.

PORTABILITY—Tools must be small and light enough to transport from store to home on foot, by bike, or by minibus.

EASE OF INSTALLATION AND USE—Tools must be easy to set up and use, without additional tools or training.

STRENGTH AND DURABILITY—Our tools are used in harsh conditions and will be pushed to their limits. They must be built to withstand abuse. We offer a one-year guarantee on all of our products.

DESIGN FOR AVAILABLE MANUFACTURING CAPACITY—Mass production keeps cost down, but locally available materials and processes can dictate the design.

CULTURAL ACCEPTABILITY—Local cultures will not change to adopt a new technology; the technology has to be adapted to local customs.

ENVIRONMENTAL SUSTAINABILITY—Our tools must not create a negative impact on the environment.

ONE LAPTOP PER CHILD

What is the One Laptop per Child project? What are its goals?

NN: Its name speaks for itself. The goal is to bring education to the poorest children in the most remote parts of the world (fig. 1).

Why do you consider One Laptop per Child an educational initiative? Do you think closing the digital divide is really a literacy and education problem?

NN: Almost every problem, from war to poverty, is solved, in part, through education. The so-called digital divide is no different than the Mercedes divide. Market economies will lean to the high-end, high-margin product, the early adopters, and then trickle down to the masses. Only when the high-end is saturated, like in the cell-phone industry, do people look at emerging markets because, what can I say, they are new "markets."

How was this project initially conceived? What was your inspiration?

NN: This is almost forty years of work. It started in the late 1960s, founded on the principles espoused by Seymour Papert. His early work on "teaching children thinking" led to Logo. In the 1980s, he and I worked in Senegal, Colombia, and Costa Rica. In the 1990s, we engaged in telecommunications projects using what is now called Wi-Fi and WiMAX. Telecommunications is not the problem any longer because there are so many concurrent paths to low-cost broadband.

Furthermore, it is elastic, in that a given bandwidth can serve fifty, sixty, or seventy children. As soon as you want, and believe in, one laptop per child, it is not elastic. Ten more children require ten more laptops. Projects in Cambodia and Maine led to OLPC as we know it today.

Why do you think it is important to provide this kind of technology at this point in time?

NN: Because it is just now possible; it was not as little as one year ago. Furthermore, the world just cannot train teachers and expect that to scale rapidly. Don't stop doing that, but it will take a very long time if you do that only. We need to leverage the children themselves. Drop a Playstation or GameBoy in the middle of the jungle into the hands of a child who has never seen electricity. The first thing he or she will do is discard the manual and start using it.

How do you see the laptop being used by the students?

NN: It will be used for almost everything, at home and at school, for music and for reading. It will be used in so many ways that our vision right now is irrelevant. What it will *not* be used for is so-called "productivity software"—Word, Excel, and PowerPoint—not because these are faulty products, but because those things are not what children need to do. Children need to make things, communicate with other children, and explore the world. They are not little office workers. We have no interest in kids learning so-called IT. Our aim is for them to learn learning. "Learning learning" is Seymour Papert's expression, and says it all.

INTERVIEW WITH NICHOLAS NEGROPONTE, FOUNDER AND CHAIRMAN OF OLPC, AND YVES BÉHAR, FUSEPROJECT, DESIGNER OF OLPC

BY CYNTHIA SMITH

1. One Laptop per Child, ¾ front view with antenna ears up, Nigerian green and white.

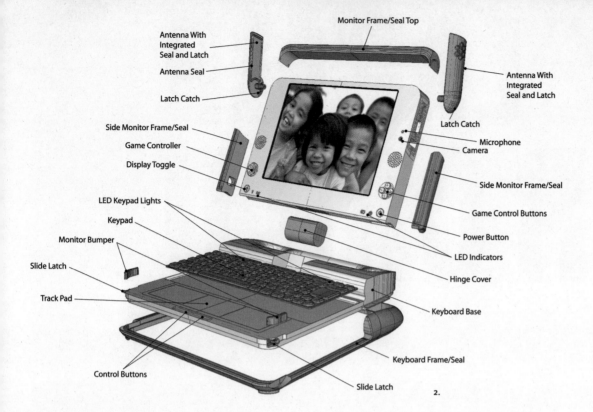

Antenna With Integrated Seal and Latch

Antenna Seal

Latch Catch

Side Monitor Frame/Seal

Game Controller

Display Toggle

LED Keypad Lights

Keypad

Monitor Bumper

Slide Latch

Track Pad

Control Buttons

Slide Latch

Monitor Frame/Seal Top

Antenna With Integrated Seal and Latch

Latch Catch

Microphone

Camera

Side Monitor Frame/Seal

Game Control Buttons

Power Button

LED Indicators

Hinge Cover

Keyboard Base

Keyboard Frame/Seal

2.

How did you keep the laptop's price so low? Why is it only available through large government initiatives?

NN: The price is lowered in three ways:

1) We have no sales, marketing, distribution, or profit, and that cuts out about half of the cost of any laptop on the market.

2) We have invented a less expensive—and, we think, better—display technology.

3) We do not use Windows, but Linux, which means a small computational footprint and free software.

Why did you decide to create a laptop and not a desktop computer?

NN: Because the child needs a seamless experience, more book-like and more personal. Ownership of the laptop is key (figs. 3, 5). Also, imagine a country whose language did not have writing and the elders invented it. Can you then imagine putting one pencil at the back of each classroom or suggesting a special room with twenty pencils, called a writing lab? We can move beyond that.

How does this laptop differ from the traditional idea of a laptop?

Three differences:

1) Dual-mode display, sunlight readable, as well as not transmissive.

2) Low power consumption, thus can be wind-up (or other human power).

3) Mesh network that can connect all the laptops so hundreds of children can share a single, back-haul connection to the Internet.

Explain the evolution of the design and the final components.

YB: I received this question recently about the One Laptop per Child project: "Why is design so important on the $100 laptop? Isn't design a bit of luxury for a product destined for the developing world?"

This typical Western view misses the point completely: quality and values are universally understood! How dare we think that people living in conditions less ideal than ours do not understand, expect, or deserve the same high standards of design?

Typically, projects for the developing world are hand-me-down versions of Western products: lesser technologies and of lesser quality. Low-cost products are literally cheap (low-tech and low quality). This is the paradigm Nicholas Negroponte, the MIT team, and the designers at fuseproject want to change. For the $100 laptop, low cost means high-tech *and* high design—a true departure. The OLPC has a low price, but high technology—some of them not found on current high-end laptops—and high design.

Why is design important? Because design brings incredible value to the function, experience, and feel of this object, and specifically, a design that is robust, high-touch, and expressive at the same time. Upon experiencing a prototype, Bono spoke of the very real meaning OLPC will have for the kids: dignity and pride to now possess their own education, communication, and entertainment tool.

We believe this project will not only change the lives of the kids that use it, but it will also change computer technology. For the first time, true cutting-edge technological solutions are blended with high-touch design for a very low price.

The $100 laptop is designed as a compact, durable, and expressive product. When closed, the entire unit is sealed, protecting it from dust and dirt, and when it is opened, it has a whimsical and tactile richness, with the Wi-Fi antennae (also called Rabbit Ears) (fig. 4) giving the OLPC a personality.

Everything on the laptop serves at least two purposes, giving it a sense of economy and efficiency: The antennae also function as covers for the laptop's USB ports and as dual latches to close the clamshell. The handle doubles as an attachment for a shoulder strap. The surrounding colored bumper is at once a seal to protect from dust and a tactile ergonomic palm surface, and it integrates the feet on the underside of the laptop. The screen is both a colored image screen and a high-contrast black and white screen for reading text, even in the sun. In eBook mode, the wide-track pad doubles as a drawing/stencil writing tablet—important for learning to write script letters (fig. 2).

With the powerful built-in Wi-Fi antennas, children will be able to connect with each other, their schools, and to the Web. The mesh network is possible thanks to these antennae: they achieve half-a-mile radius, which connects laptops to one another. This is also possible since the school districts will distribute literally one unit per child, hence disseminating many Wi-Fi spots across a town or village and instantly creating a Wi-Fi network for entire areas. Servers and satellite connections are dropped in remote places, allowing the kids to connect from anywhere and access school books and lessons from the school directly. In places where an Internet connection already exists, no server will be needed.

Skype, Google, Echostar, and Linux Red Hat are some of the more visible partners, and, thanks to an integrated video camera, microphone, and the powerful Wi-Fi antennae, children will be able to connect readily.

Traditional power and human-power solutions include rechargeable batteries, hand cranks, foot pedals, pull cords, and, eventually, solar energy, depending on the appropriate need. Because the OLPC software requires low processing power, the hardware consumes very little energy—two watts in full operational mode, 0.25 watt in mesh-network standby mode. The OLPC is extremely energy-efficient.

fuseproject is trying to create a computer revolution for the children of the world. This is a rare creative project, as designers are mostly concerned with, and their work experienced by, one billion people in the world (the so-called West), while the OLPC could touch the other six billion people that make up our planet. From a technology and information-access standpoint, OLPC accomplishes what the personal computer was supposed to do in the first place: bring access to information to all.

What kinds of software applications will run on the laptop? Why did you choose these applications?

NN: Everything. We will provide constructionist tools, like Logo and eToys. But many applications will run on it. It has an SD card slot and three USB plugs for DVD, hard disc, printer, etc. It has a built-in camera of its own.

Explain why you chose to use open-source software on the laptop. What are the implications globally for taking this direction?

NN: Open source is the flip side of the OLPC coin. Among other reasons, we use open source in order to localize the laptop. There is no alternative. The global implication is that Linux will expand to the desktop, where it has very little presence today, in spite of open source being about half of the server market.

The first concept had a very distinctive hand crank to charge it, but now I understand Squid Labs has developed a new way of powering it. How will that work? How long will the charge last?

NN: Three approaches are being taken concurrently. A crank, a peddle, and the Squid Labs pull cord. The battery can last a long time—as many as twelve hours—and we do not recommend charging it by hand, although it is possible. Our goal is for human power to work at a ratio of at least one to ten—one minute of cranking gives you ten minutes of use.

Do you have plans for testing the machine in the field?

NN: We have plans galore. In fact, 500 machines will be tested to destruction. Another 500 will be tested each in Thailand, Nigeria, Brazil, Argentina, and one or two more countries to be announced. Testing started in November 2006.

I understand that you are waiting to manufacture the laptops once you have five million on order from different governments. Nigeria, the first to commit to the project, has ordered one million laptops. What other countries are interested in the laptop? When do you plan to deliver the first computers?

NN: We need a threshold to reach sufficient scale and to get a low enough cost. That number is about five million units. No country has signed, and we are asking them not to do so until we test.

Former UN Secretary General Kofi Annan remarked, "[OLPC] holds the promise of major advances in economic and social development. But perhaps most important is the true meaning of one laptop per child. This is not just a matter of giving a laptop to each child, as if bestowing on them some magical charm. The magic lies within: within each child, within each scientist, scholar, or just plain citizen in the making." Despite his glowing statement, this project has been controversial. Some critics have said that if one went to families in the developing country and asked them what they needed, a laptop would not be first on their list. Food, water, and electricity may be more of a priority for them. One education minister thinks his country's resources would be better put to use building classrooms and hiring teachers "more urgently than fancy tools." How do you respond to these criticisms?

NN: We do not respond to these criticisms. The project will speak for itself. Imagine telling some of those same ministers ten years ago that cell phones or the Internet would be ubiquitous. Time to stop arguing, and whoever wants to do this does it. A lot of the criticism you hear comes from large commercial interests who have provided several governments with misinformation. We have caught them red-handed doing so. It is pretty sad.

Often more problems are created when the developed world provides technology for those without it. How will your organization provide for a sustainable support for the new users?

NN: Sustainable is a word that does not always apply. Sidewalks, clean air, and basic health services are not always sustainable unto themselves, but rather part of a bigger social picture and civic responsibility. Basic education is, too. Even the poorest country will spend $100 per year per child on primary education. Add $30 a year, and that is a big jump. But most developing countries spend more like $500. So this is not such a big deal.

What do think the likely impact will be in providing these laptops to children in the developing world? Do you think this project will help alleviate poverty in the communities that will receive them?

NN: Big, and yes.

Is this project only for the developing world, or will you also address the needs of children here in the United States and other developed countries who do not have access to a computer?

NN: This project is for the developing world. Period. It may expand to include the developed world in a way that subsidizes the poorer countries. Sure, there is poverty in every country, but our mission is to go to the extremes and design a different organization, a different laptop, a different form of connectivity, and a different educational plan.

What if the project fails?

NN: Failure has no downside in our case. If it fails tomorrow, it has already had an industry impact. If it fails in a year, it may be because the laptop costs $150 and cannot come out for six months. Those would be very soft landings. Also, keep in mind that we do not have shareholders. Our stakeholders are the kids. We are determined not to let them down.

5. OLPC, ¾ front view with book strap.

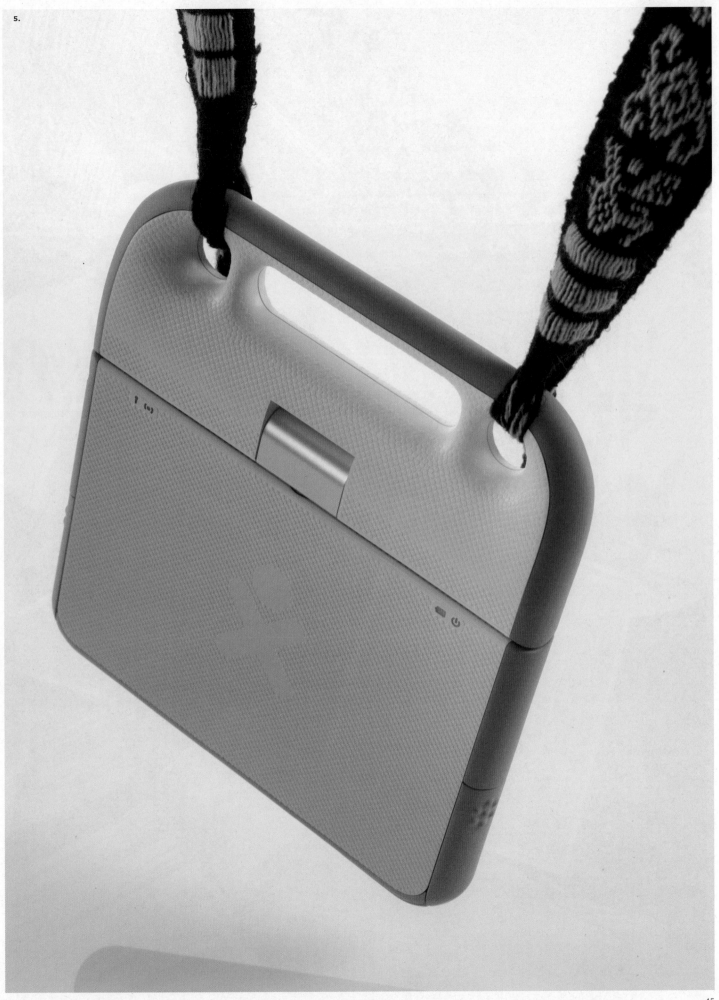

RELIABLE, RENEWABLE RURAL ENERGY

H. HARISH HANDE

A reliable source of energy is rare for India's rural inhabitants. Over half of India's population of 1.1 billion has no access to electricity; and one hundred million households lack modern energy sources for cooking. The majority of its population also does not have the power to undertake income-generating activities or run small businesses.

For the underserved, the best options for reliable energy are decentralized, clean, and renewable options, such as solar power, biogas, etc. Paradoxically, however, the people who are most in need of alternate energy options cannot afford or efficiently utilize presently available systems. Innovative products, linkages, and finance programs are needed to create more opportunities for the country's lower-income groups to access these alternate sources and raise their quality of life. SELCO India's aim is to be a catalyst for this change.

Along with Neville Williams, founder and head of the U.S.-based nonprofit organization Solar Electric Light Fund (SELF), I founded SELCO in Bangalore, India, in 1995 to help the country's poor afford and maintain sustainable energy technologies, as well as to dispel the myth that social ventures cannot be run as commercial entities.

SELCO is the first rural-based company in India to concentrate on marketing and servicing solar home-lighting systems as a means to provide small amounts of reliable power to underserved households. We partner with numerous financial institutions, microfinance groups, non-government organizations (NGOS), cooperatives, and other groups with missions to empower the poor and make this technology affordable and accessible. Over the last eleven years, we have installed solar lighting systems in 65,000 households (fig. 1) in rural India, as well as helped the local economy by employing local labor to maintain these systems.

A key way to alleviate poverty is to create income-generating opportunities for the poor. These activities require energy services; and, in turn, these services and finished goods need to be financed by local financial institutions. SELCO plays a critical role in each link of the development chain—providing the technology for the specific energy need and helping to create the appropriate financing mechanism to support the various ventures.

From the beginning, SELCO India has focused on creating solutions appropriate for the needs of the end users, primarily for rural households and small businesses, whether they are connected to a grid or without electricity entirely. For those without reliable electricity, the Solar Home System replaces sources such as kerosene for wick lamps, dry-cell batteries for flashlights and radios, car batteries for lighting and television, and, at the higher end, diesel or gasoline generator sets. This alternative energy system provides lighting or direct power to a wide range of enterprise clients, including grocery shops, tailors, poultry farms and cattle ranches, sericulture farms, saw and rice mills, electronics-repair shops, and public calling centers (figs. 2-4).

In the late 1990s, we began concentrating on income-generating applications involving productive uses of lighting, extended business hours for rural stores, or energy used directly for sewing machines and soldering irons.

1. Solar panels being installed by SELCO technicians for a rural house in Sri Lanka.

2. Street hawker shifted from kerosene lamps to solar lights, which were financed by the local financial institution, Udupi, Karnataka, India.

3. Light system for a mathematics class, Dharwad, Karnataka, India.

4. Better lights in a roadside tea stall have attracted clients, Mandarti Village, Karnataka State, India.

Financing the solar electric system is a must for those who most need this energy and light—impoverished families. However, a basic system can cost as much as three months' to a year's income. SELCO pioneered innovative consumer-loan programs with Malaprabha Grameen Bank, a rural bank. Connecting end users in rural areas with third-party micro-credit and rental options made the product affordable. We have mobilized an estimated $10 million with our financing partners.

SELCO's target for the next five years is to provide 200,000 underserved families and businesses with reliable energy services. We will continue to base our activities on the belief that, in rural energy delivery, technology is easy. The true challenge is to continue to find ways to improve prospects for our customers while ensuring that all links in the development chain are financially sound.

ROLLING WATER

Millions of people all over the world, especially in rural Africa, live many kilometers from a reliable source of clean water, leaving them vulnerable to cholera, dysentery, and other water-borne diseases. We have all seen pictures of women and children in developing countries carrying heavy containers of water, mostly on their heads; this labor invariably causes many neck and spine injuries.

The idea for the Q Drum originated as a way for rural people to ease the burden of carrying clean and potable water. The solution had to be simple; water in any meaningful quantity is too heavy to carry. Rolling the water—not lifting or carrying it—in a cylindrical container seemed to be the only viable solution, and the container had to be durable in areas where even a hammer or a nail is a scarce commodity.

The uniqueness of the Q Drum lies in the design of the longitudinal shaft, or doughnut hole, which permits the drum to be pulled along using a rope run through the hole (fig. 1). There are no removable or breakable handles or axles, and the rope can be replaced by means available everywhere, such as a leather thong or a rope woven from plant material. The drum is manufactured from polyethylene through rotational molding, and has a high compatibility with foodstuffs and water. Its durability has been proven by extensive actual use in rural areas of southern Africa. One such seventy-five-liter container showed very little wear and tear after more than eight years of daily use.

The Q Drum has transformed the centuries-old labor of fetching water into something akin to fun. More water can be transported per journey with considerably less effort; even a child can pull a fifty-liter drum over flat terrain for several kilometers without undue strain. This could shift the burden of water collection away from adult women to children (figs. 2, 3), thereby leaving the women free to do other important work. Moreover, by not carrying these heavy and unstable loads on their heads, users can avoid many injuries (figs. 4, 5).

Although every effort has been made to keep the price of the Q Drum as low as possible, it is still unaffordable to most people—those who need it cannot afford it, and those who can do not need it. If marketing and distribution of the product were solely dependent on charity, the project would not be sustainable. However, if it is properly funded by international donors, non-governmental organizations, and private corporations, the Q Drum can contribute to making life a lot easier for rural communities in Africa and elsewhere in the world for future generations to come.

PIETER HENDRIKSE

1. The Q Drum, Pietersburg, South Africa.

2. Boy pulling a Q Drum with relative ease, Village of Nobody, (near Pietersburg) South Africa.

3. Woman pulling the Q Drum, Village of Nobody, South Africa.

4. Women and children collecting water in plastic containers, Village of Nobody, South Africa.

5. Two tired women using the traditional method. In poorer areas these heavy containers are carried on the heads causing many neck and spine injuries, Village of Nobody near Pietersburg.

INFORMAL COMMUNITY SOLAR
KITCHENS

Informal urban settlements—what we used to call squatter communities—have significantly transformed the urban landscape of Mexico since the 1960s. They remain a very present reminder of the effects of globalization on this rapidly modernizing country. Some cities, including many which border the United States, have been so consumed by these settlements that they are no longer distinguishable from them. These communities lack a basic physical infrastructure, with little clean water or paved roads, poor sewage systems, no local schools or governmental systems, and other serious problems.

Along with these physical transformations of the urban landscape come massive shifts in Mexico's social fabric. For every two migrant workers that come to the United States, one woman is left behind with the family's children, in addition to those too poor, sick, or old to make the journey. These and other related circumstances can cause tremendous strain on the life of a community and its residents, calling into question its ultimate physical and cultural sustainability. Despite the cultural fragmentation and pressure that occur, longstanding community traditions of building remain the backbone of these informal settlements. These traditions, along with an eagerness for community empowerment, are indispensable resources for positive future development.

1. The Solar Kitchen perches itself on preexisting terraces to allow more room for the little playspace that existed.

2004–05 JOSE MARIA MORELOS SOLAR KITCHEN

SERGIO PALLERONI

In 2004, BASIC Initiative, a collaboration of faculty and students from Penn State University, the University of Washington, and other universities, returned for its twelfth project in the communities of Tejalpa-Jiutepec, two traditional villages which have grown twelve-fold in a decade, due to the arrival of poor farmers no longer able to compete with the global economies of farming. The project, a solar kitchen, was a retrofit to the Jose Maria Morelos School (fig. 1), built a decade earlier by one of the many informal communities that now make up Tejalpa and Jiutepec. At the southernmost edge of the communities we have been working with since the late 1980s, the school is built upon the agricultural terraces which the indigenous people of the region cultivated for the last four thousand years. In this hillside location, on leftover land—which is often the condition of many of the public works we have built in this growing squatter community—the school's buildings left little play space for its 360 elementary-school children (fig. 4).

The previous year, we had experimented with a design for a solar condenser stove and oven for the kitchen of another elementary school, a kilometer away. The design of the earlier collector, based on German engineering by Solaird, had been adapted through a counterweight, much like a grandfather clock, to track the sun. Basically built from bicycle parts for the mechanism and small vanity mirrors bought cheaply at the local street market for the parabolic mirror surface, the solar parabolic mirror concentrates the energy of the sun on a pot or stove in the

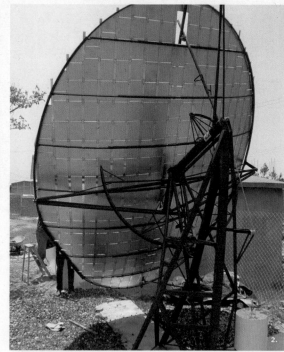

kitchen (fig. 2). Though complicated in appearance, the device is a simple and inexpensive way to harness the sun's energy to help reduce the cost of cooking meals for the children of these schools. Cooking meals for their children is one of the ways the mothers of the community have organized themselves to both supplement the diets of their children and reduce costs (fig. 3). That the schools, which are run by the federal government (even when the community is often forced to build its own schools in these communities) had agreed to allow the mothers on school grounds to cook for their children had been a major policy victory for Comunidad AC, the not-for-profit organization we have been working with for almost two decades. Now the challenge was to rethink the idea of the kitchen as an ecological response to the needs and conditions of the squatter community (fig. 5).

The students in our program took on the challenge of the solar kitchen as a means to rethink not only the energy requirements of a traditional kitchen but also its use of water, toilets, and lighting, as well as an opportunity to im-

pact nutrition and homebuilding in the community. In other words, they reformulated the challenge of the schools' kitchens to affect change in the homes of the parents whose children attended the school. In their analysis of the community, the students found that the kitchens had a great deal of ecological impact on this rapidly growing settlement. The design of the kitchen reflected these concerns with its incorporation of alternative, non-polluting, economical technologies like solar cooking, solar water heating, graywater filters to treat the dishwater, and natural light as the main source of lighting. The addition of an open dining pavilion allowed the students to also incorporate rainwater catchment and PV panels to take the kitchen essentially off the grid.

There are three prototype solar kitchens already in operation in the Tejalpa-Jiutepec communities, and the local municipal government, at the residents' urging, has agreed to fund the construction of several more in the next few years (fig. 6).

2. The first solar dish, showing counterweighted mechanism built from bicycle parts.

3. Before the Solar Kitchen, mothers prepared lunches for their children on the street.

4. The existing school, constructed out of leftover land and pre-existing agricultural terraces.

5. The interior of the Solar Kitchen, lit by skylights and natural light, a requirement of the program.

6. The Solar Kitchen, now more of a community center for this impoverished community, stands as a beacon at night above the community. United States, 1987.

LIFE LINE

In the northeastern United States, deer devour tulips in the spring before we get to enjoy them. In Connecticut, where I live, porcupines eat apples and pears from our trees, wild turkeys eat every last blueberry, and, once a season or so, a black bear raids the birdfeeders. People with gardens spend a lot of energy trying to outsmart the local wildlife. Mostly we fail.

But imagine if our gardens were the only source of our family's food and income. Imagine if our lives depended on what they produced, and the local wildlife raiding our gardens were hungry, desperate, six-ton elephants. In one evening, a single elephant can easily trample and eat an entire year's worth of crops; and they usually travel in herds.

In the few places left in the world where elephants live in the wild, illegal logging and the increasing human population encroach on their habitat, forcing them to wander in search of food (fig. 1). The greatest threat to the survival of elephants in the wild is no longer poaching—though that is, tragically, still rampant—it is the loss of their habitat.

Human-elephant conflict can be deadly. In Kenya, elephants have killed 200 people and injured many more over the past seven years. In return, between fifty and 120 elephants are shot each year by wildlife authorities. The situation is the same wherever elephants come into conflict with people. Scientists at the World Wildlife Fund have taken on the challenge of mitigating this conflict. Finding a peaceful solution has been a major challenge requiring patience, keen observation, and invention. As strong, smart, and persistent as elephants are, it turns out they have an Achilles' heel. They don't like spicy food.

A chili fence is a simple hemp rope soaked in hot chili oil and engine grease. Strung up around a garden, it stings an elephant's sensitive hide, and is the first line of defense in this fight for survival (fig. 2). Of course the battle frequently doesn't end there. If the chili fence fails, a chili bomb (chili oil and dung, lit on fire and hurled in the elephant's direction) is the next alternative.

WWF has been teaching these techniques to communities in parts of Asia and Africa. The results have been impressive, including a dramatic reduction in lost crops and lives, and better nutrition. In one village, chili bombs so irritated a bull elephant that he turned and ran off, leading the rest of the herd with him. The raiders stayed away for five weeks—long enough for the villagers to harvest mangoes for the first time in ten years.

Lasting solutions to this problem, and the core of WWF's plan, are to curtail illegal logging and help ensure that land is zoned and managed so that humans can develop sustainable livelihoods and wildlife can live peacefully alongside them.

The divergent needs of impoverished people and the natural world can appear, at first, to be irreconcilable. Enlightened people and organizations know that these problems must be solved concurrently, or not at all. This simple rope represents that enlightenment.

1. Herd of Indian elephants (*Elephas maximus bengalensis*) in Rajaji National Park, northern India.

2. Bennety Busihu (left), field officer of the IRDNC, and Cordelia Muyoba (right), project manager of the Kwandu Conservancy, inspecting the chili plot together with the owner of the plot, Kwandu Conservancy, East Caprivi, Namibia, February 2006.

CHERYL HELLER

LEAPFROG:
DESIGN STRATEGIES FOR GLOBAL
INNOVATION

SHEILA KENNEDY

"Leapfrog" technology is a term often used to describe an advance in technology that is so sudden and decisive that it appears to bypass or jump over historical patterns of gradual development. Yet the analogy of a frog's leap forward is misleading. Creating a new idea which challenges prevailing practices and implementing that idea in real conditions "on the ground" involve the imagination of a reverse trajectory in time. Imagine first where the frog will land, locate what could happen in that future place, and form an understanding of it. Then take that knowledge back into the present in order to identify the obstacles that stand in the way of that future, and design a way forward. Rather than a grand leap, this often happens in a series of small and sometimes stealthy hops, each of which causes a positive disruption in the pattern established by present conditions.

The Portable Light project began with an idea—as much a leap of faith as of the imagination—that there could, and should, be an intersection between design research and social action. The work of MATx, the material-research unit of KVA, was focused on the exploration of design strategies for the integration of semiconductor materials into textiles, building materials, and architecture (fig. 1). Energy-efficient light-emitting diodes produce bright, cool light with very small amounts of electricity; photovoltaic materials convert sunlight into electricity. The trajectory for-

1. Portable Light reading mat in standing screen position to show potential applications for schoolchildren in rural areas. Designer: Portable Light team, KVA MATx.

ward was to ask what might be the useful connections between the emerging potentials of flexible electronics, the existing capabilities of computer-driven design and manufacturing, and the urgent need for a new type of self-contained infrastructure which could provide useful amounts of electrical light and power to the very large number of people—more than two billion—who do not have access to electricity.

By necessity, the project needed to fill several major criteria: Such an infrastructure could not be based on the dominant model of the centralized electrical grid and the building-integrated electrical system. It needed to be fully autonomous and simple enough to be reliable. The lighting system needed to be lightweight to reduce transport costs and rugged enough to ship and use without breaking. Its elements needed to last for several years with components that could be easily replaced, remade, or recycled. It needed to be highly affordable and versatile so that it could be adapted for many purposes in different cultures. The size and form of the system needed to be flexible enough to incorporate changes over time, collapse for shipping, and expand again for use. Lastly, this new form of infrastructure had to be capable of producing a wholly different set of effects so that its users would make a connection with this technology and want to care for it and make it their own.

These performance characteristics served as advance criteria for the design of Portable Light and provided a new perspective from which to ask what could be done right now with what we already had. As a renewable and distributed system, each Portable Light unit is a self-contained light engine that generates its own power in a

2. Energy-harvesting bag, woven with back-strap loom. Designer: Estela Hernandez and her daughter, using Portable Light flexible electronics designed by the Portable Light team at KVA MATx, Sierra Madre, Mexico.

flexible, adaptable textile form. Portable Light combines high-brightness light-emitting diodes (HBLEDs) from pedestrian walk signals, water-resistant tactile switches from dishwashers, and rechargeable batteries from cell phones. These components were deliberately sourced from familiar "first-world" consumer appliances and standard technologies with well defined, large-volume commercial markets. Existing economies of scale were then leveraged by showing manufacturers how their standard, low-cost technology products could gain additional value in the new space of an adjacent "needs-based" market for Portable Light.

Here, innovation became the art of creating both a different perception of value within the technology industry and a set of digital bridging technologies that optimize the efficient performance of these seemingly unrelated components with energy-harvesting photovoltaic panels. This approach can be understood as an expanded form of material misuse,[1] a creative amnesia which allows "ordinary" technology components to be reimagined in different pieces, packages, and relationships (fig. 2). The potentials of this idea are not lost on an emerging generation of designers, who are not content to consume technology, but instead choose to upload, unpack, hack, hybridize, and reconfigure their software and hardware.

Portable Light was designed to be small, smart, and stealthy. Rather than wait for the semiconductor lighting technology to mature or become market-ready, the design team asked how can small amounts of light and power could become an advantage for this project. Digital

electronics, designed to stretch the system's finite limits of capacity, tripled the relationship of run time to charge time, and protocols for distributed intelligence were created to allow multiple Portable Light units to charge together faster in a group than they would individually.[2] Portable Light allows for rapid implementation with less expense associated with overland and air transportation.

As a completely portable and personalized system, it is efficient and effective. Units can be carried with their owners to provide access to light and power when needed. Since needs are often urgent, Portable Light is small enough to be agile in implementation. The rechargeable cell-phone batteries of Portable Light are not caught up in the morass of international shipping and customs regulations that can impede the transportation of conventional batteries required for larger silicon-based solar-power systems.

As a "common-denominator" material familiar in many cultures, the textile form of Portable Light presented a possible way to engage the participation of women in the stewardship and use of this lighting technology, because women often perform much of the labor in rural communities and are among the most vulnerable in traditional cultures. Working in collaboration with the non-governmental organization Centro Huichol and the Rocky Mountain Institute, the first Portable Light pilot project was initiated to serve the needs of the Wixarika (Huichol), an indigenous semi-nomadic people who live in remote regions of the Mexican Sierra Madre Occidental. In the Sierra, access to light means much more than the absence of darkness. Light

provides the Huichol with access to a group of key social resources; it is a beginning point which enables communities to have options for education and industry, and it improves the level of medical care that doctors and first responders can provide in these remote areas.

In the Huichol village of Nuevo Colonia, children walk down from the mountains each Sunday to spend a week at the government-run elementary school. Standing in the dormitory of closely packed metal bunk beds, each with nothing more than a bare mattress, the schoolteacher says that the children are better off here than in their family *ranchos* in the high Sierra, because at school they are fed twice a day. Looking at the dark, leaky, and reeking cement bathrooms, it is not hard to imagine why the children prefer to wash in the river, even though the water is not clean. The two schoolteachers, one Mexican, one Huichol, want to provide each child with Portable Light to prevent the accidents that occur on the steep mountain roads at night and to provide illumination to study with when the children work with their families and are not able to come to school.

Many Huichol men and families travel each year from the Sierra to the coast of Nayarit, where as day laborers in the tobacco plantations they are exposed to largely unregulated, toxic agricultural chemicals.[3] The opportunity to have Portable Light to work in the evening in their ranchos is welcome, for reasons of health, family welfare, and economics. In the Sierra, access to light translates directly into the improved ability for a family to increase its income. This is especially important for women, who are often the single

heads of large households (fig. 3). The Huichol shape the light to their particular needs, using the textile surfaces to provide direct, reflected, or diffuse lighting, as needed for cottage-based industries such as community *tortillerías*, sandal making, repair work, weaving, and beading.

Basic health problems, infant mortality, and malnutrition are very high among community members in the Sierra. Of the 806 majority indigenous communities in Mexico, eighty-three percent are classified by the International Relations Center as high or very high marginality, meaning they live in extreme poverty. Malnutrition is among the leading causes of death for the Huichol.[4] Susanna Valadez, the unconventional director of the Centro Huichol, who works with the Portable Light team and the international aid organization Plenty, maintains that ,with a localized light in their cabins, women are able to prepare nutritious meals for their families instead of giving them the expensive and less nutritious instant meals sold in the stores of the foothill villages.[5] In addition, Portable Light provides a measure of basic health and safety, as women can spot the *alacran*, the poisonous scorpions of the Sierra, brush them off the walls, and kill them. The stings of these scorpions are very painful for adults and often kill babies and small children who sleep in the ranchos.

Prototypes developed by the Portable Light team in collaboration with members of the Huichol community[6] have demonstrated how small amounts of light and power can make a big difference in the lives of people who have so little. Yet with the benefits of Portable Light comes a

set of dilemmas we have observed through our direct experiences of this project. These problems are useful, as they help to put into question our assumptions about the distribution of power, in every sense of the word.

Is it really a surprise to find that the Huichol already have a name, *taweami*, or firefly, and a way of understanding light-emitting materials within the history and traditions of their culture?[7] Or that the uses the Huichol make of digital light and the conditions of the Sierra might offer an instructive perspective and expand the realm of applications and material possibilities for this portable technology? The schoolteacher wants to use Portable Light to charge the battery of her cell phone. The doctor wants to carry Portable Light with her to assist women in the many difficult *partidos*. The river suggests that the solid-state technology in Portable Light could purify a cup of water or sterilize medical equipment. The dormitory in winter makes it clear that the by-product heat from the HBLED illumination could help keep the children's hands warm.

If women weavers prefer to produce their own integrations of Portable Light, as demonstrated by Dr. Stacy Schaefer,[8] an anthropologist who is working with Portable Light in the Wixarika communities of San Andreas, how does this change the economic equation of consumer and producer, or the question of authorship and ownership of technology? Working with kits of Portable Light electronics, women weavers have designed their own light-emitting textiles, using a back-strap loom and Mesoamerican weaving techniques more than a thousand years old (fig. 4). By integrating Portable Light into their *kuxira* (belt) or *k+tsiuri* (carry bags), Huichol women are both continuing their traditional practices and expanding their possibilities to participate as producers of technology in new economies of their own creation. These women may take ownership of the Portable Light they create. They may trade or sell it to others in their community, or produce it in woven goods for sale to tourists in Puerta Vallarta or Zacatecas (fig. 5).

In the delivery of light or electrical power, how little or how much is enough, and for whom? As a distributed and cooperative network of many small but efficient pieces, Portable Light offers an alternative to the electrical grid system and the dependencies it produces for vulnerable people through its fixed locations and monthly service fees.[9]

Confronted with real human need, the argument for providing at least a little power or light is more compelling than providing none.[10] But is it reasonable to expect that projects such as this will be able to provide an adequate level of response to long-term community needs? This question is especially poignant if, in other parts of the world, continued investment in a centralized and wasteful infrastructure goes unquestioned, even as it becomes increasingly more damaging to the global environment and costly to maintain and protect. The trajectory of influence could also be reversed by enabling projects such as Portable Light to serve as new models that could be applied to this country, opening possibilities for the integration of distributed energy into a diaspora of materials and artifacts.

The emerging recognition in this country of global needs for clean water, medical care, electricity, and education is changing the role of innovation in design and industry. As this happens, creative, strategic, and ethical thinking in design is needed as well as the courage, resiliency, and will to address large and complex problems without ready solutions. If the design disciplines, in collaboration with university research centers and manufacturing sectors, can provide provocative and pragmatic approaches to these challenges, they are poised for trajectories of practice which will bring them a new level of public impact and public scrutiny. They will become the creators of important forms of applied thought in our contemporary knowledge-based economy.

4. Estela Hernandez sewing the photovoltaics into her woven bag, San Andreas region, Sierra Madre, Mexico.

5. Detail of light-emitting bag, woven and designed by Estela Hernandez and her daughter, showing traditional K+tsiuri wiwierite (belt strap) weaving as a means of enclosing the HBLED and wireway, Sierra Madre, Mexico.

5.

KATRINA
FURNITURE PROJECT

SERGIO PALLERONI

"Because the pathway to sustainability cannot be charted in advance, it will have to be navigated through trial and error and conscious experimentation. The urgent need is to design strategies and institutions that can better integrate incomplete knowledge with experimental action into programs of adaptive management and social learning." —Bruce Alberts, President of the National Academy of Sciences[1]

In August 2005, Hurricane Katrina exposed the poverty and underdevelopment that are increasingly a part of first-world countries, and revealed the extreme economic and social inequality that exists in the United States. In a more positive light, the disaster provoked an overwhelming mobilization of students and faculty throughout the country, and design schools in particular, to the aid of the devastated region. One example of this movement is the Katrina Furniture Project, headed by the University of Texas's BASIC Initiative partnership with Design Corps, the Art Center College of Design, and the Hamer Center at Penn State University. At the heart of the project are furniture-making workshops which help train Gulf Coast residents, many of whom have lost their homes and jobs, for new economic opportunities in the community, provide reconstruction resources, and recycle a portion of the detritus (figs. 1, 3) created by Katrina (a process already begun by Mercy Corps, one of the partners in this initiative). The Katrina Furniture Project is a New Orleans–based, not-for-profit community organization, managed by the

7. A completed pew in front of First Black Baptist Church, New Orleans, LA.

affected communities for the economic and social benefit of their residents. It emphasizes design not as the isolated practice of architects, but as a complex social process through which change occurs. Community Design Fellowships from the University of Texas at Austin, Design Corps, and the Rose Fellowship will prepare young architects and students to integrate service into their professions and their lives.

The furniture-making workshops train community members in the craft of making furniture and, when necessary, in the fundamentals of operating these workshops safely and according to fundamental business models (fig. 2). The training will be led by faculty and students from participating universities and non-governmental organizations and coordinated with local arts institutions. The workshops are intended to be multipurpose in nature and function as neighborhood-based places of work, sites of learning, and community centers. Weekend workshops, for example, help provide facilities, tools, and expertise for community members trying to rebuild their homes. Organizational business plans, equipment purchases, and marketing of Katrina Furniture Workshop products will be assisted by the business schools of participating universities and by local banks and churches.

These collaborators are taking on the reconstruction of buildings donated by each community to become local Katrina Furniture Workshops. These reconstructions help build the capacity of participating neighborhoods and students as well as establish trust and channels of communication for the furniture-making workshops that will follow.

In the summer of 2006, students and faculty from the

University of Texas and the Design Center developed prototypes for three furniture pieces which addressed three immediate needs: a pew to help the more than 900 churches destroyed in the area rebuild their spaces of worship; a table to serve the permanently resettled communities in Texas, Louisiana, and Mississippi to connect with their past; and a stool to be mass-marketed by retailers such as Design Within Reach to create income for the community (figs. 4, 5, 7). All three are built from salvaged cypress or longleaf pine, two species from which much of New Orleans was built but which, despite their beauty and natural adaptation to the climate, are ending up as fill in the rush to rebuild the city. The prototypes also experiment with the capacity and qualities of each wood, which the students attempted to understand and celebrate in each piece. They are but the first generation, an important step in winning economic support for the project, which in itself will be a continuing exploration of how the area's residents can best use important local resources to rebuild their cities and their lives (fig. 6).

1, 3. The Green Project salvages and deconstructs damaged building to use elsewhere in the city, New Orleans, LA, 2006.

2. The process of making even the simplest elements, such as Japanese-style stepstools/boxes, involved developing an understanding of the qualities of cypress and the other woods from which New Orleans was built.

4. Japanese-style boxes on the roots of a southern oak tree, New Orleans, LA.

5. A table made of salvaged nineteenth-century old-growth cypress wood, New Orleans, LA.

6. Salvaged nineteenth-century barge boards tell the story of New Orleans and the Mississippi, New Orleans, LA.

LESSONS FROM THE MARGINALIZED:
A MANIFESTO FOR A TRULY PUBLIC ARCHITECTURE

JOHN PETERSON

Though projects such as Frank Gehry's Solomon R. Guggenheim Museum in Bilbao, Spain, have thrust architecture into the limelight of popular culture, the relevance of architecture in the contemporary urban dynamic remains limited at best. With the exception of a few efforts within the academic realm, this profession exists primarily as a service industry, waiting on clients to approach with commissions and constrained by an economic model which seldom encourages innovation or risk beyond the rigidly defined goals of the clients. In such a model, the focus becomes the pursuit of producing "architecture for architecture's sake." This ideology is noticeably disengaged from the public realm, where a multiplicity of identities, constantly evolving social structures, and often competing economic and political forces require architects to undertake the complicated issues that their profession is reluctant to confront.

There have been times in the past when the profession believed that it had a role to play in the social sphere: social treatises and agendas were key elements of the modern architecture movement, and again in the social advocacy movements of the 1960s and 1970s. Yet both epochs yielded more failures than successes in this regard. With Modernism came public housing and urban renewal. And both have come to be derided as having had detrimental effects on the modern city and the profession's relevance. In the aftermath of these large-scale design initiatives, the sixties and seventies witnessed the emergence of "advocacy" or "participatory" planning, in which design was undertaken from "the bottom up." In the quest to include all community stakeholders in the planning and design process, architects ceded a great deal of their responsibilities to achieve consensus, and thereby distanced themselves from the failures of the previous decade. Designs did not become better, more holistic urban elements which synthesized multiple, overlapping identities, but rather disparate collages, loosely joining together the needs and desires of various constituencies.

The failure of these past efforts does not relieve architects of the responsibility to seek out and act for change or progressive solutions. As we witness an increasing stratification along social, economic, and political lines, notions of space—particularly public space—become all the more significant. It has also become increasingly clear that traditional architectural forms often prove to be inadequate in addressing new social structures and the needs they present.

It is in this context that Public Architecture has emerged. Our organization's mission is to establish a new model for architectural practice by working for the common good through unique and collaborative ventures unconstrained by conventional architectural practice. To us, the more interesting, and pressing, situations are those in which the client must be identified. These are the clients who have no voice, stakeholders who have been marginalized by the contemporary urban condition. And yet their lack of a voice does not mean they are any less entitled to the benefits of a healthier public experience. Embarking on this realm of socially engaged architec-

1. Roberto: "Hace falta el ingles. Es lo mas importante en conseguir trabajo." ("I don't know English, and it's the most important thing you need to get work.")

ture, we are mindful of the lessons of the past. The social Modernist architects approached the urban landscape with the notion that architecture could create a utopia, resolving some of the social and economic ills of the modern city. Their inclination to the social responsibility of architecture was correct, but their belief in the ability of architecture to resolve these immense issues on its own was not. The subsequent participatory approach to design did not fail because of the inclusion of a public voice, but because the designers ceded their own voice—and thus their expertise—in favor of compromise, and because of a misguided interpretation of professional service.

It is in this context that Public Architecture tackles a project like the Day Labor Station. It is estimated that there are more than 117,000 day laborers looking for work each day in the United States. Though the majority of these workers are male and of Hispanic descent, the day-laborer population encompasses many ethnic groups as well as both sexes. Given the increase in the number of day-laborer sites nationally, it would seem that this population has been increasing. This increase is not just reflective of rising immigration, but also of the increased demand for low-wage labor in the critical industries of the American economy, such as construction and agriculture. The lives and work of day laborers have been largely invisible, operating in an informal economy outside the purview of official recognition. The current immigration debate has changed this, and thrust this population into the limelight. However, the newfound attention on this population has not rendered them visible in the context of public space. Day laborers are still considered a singular mass, connected with a hot-button issue. They remain faceless, and thus, without a voice.

It is for the faceless and the voiceless that we worked with photographer Elena Dorfman as part of our ongoing research. Through her striking photographs, we seek to engage the individual day laborer. Instead of an unknown member of a nondescript group, we want to call attention to day laborers as individuals with tangible needs, beliefs,

and desires (figs. 1-5). Oddly enough, it is not the places where day laborers work that have become the spaces of conflict, but rather the places in which they go to seek work. Images of street corners, gas stations, and Home Depot parking lots flood our screens and newspapers. For the most part, these day-laborer sites do not have a physical presence, other than that formed by the gathering of laborers and potential employers. In recent years, there have been efforts by a few municipalities and nonprofits to create official day-laborer centers, often based on the "union hall" model, which allow the day-laborer system to become more codified. Yet these places have had mixed success, partly because the designs and construction rarely employ the voices of the laborers themselves, and thus lack a sense of ownership; and rarely are they based on the existing social and professional structures of the day laborers (fig. 6). In proposing the Day Labor Station, Public Architecture is identifying the day laborer, not a municipal entity or a nonprofit, as its client. As such, we acknowledge their individual and collective voices—their realities, their needs, and their desires. The social structure which forms the underpinnings of their lives is not viewed as an appendage that will adapt to whatever structure is built, but instead an armature on which the design is based (fig. 7). With this perspective, and with further research and creative exploration, Public Architecture seeks to provide an institutional, spatial visibility to the day laborers, and engage the debate around their presence in a new light.

It has been written by South African architect Iain Low that every building can be a manifesto, "a declaration of what is possible." With projects such as the Day Labor Station, Public Architecture argues that this philosophy applies not only to buildings, but to all spaces. When architects commit themselves to operating in the public realm with a belief in the inclusive responsibility to affect our complex societal structures, the possibilities for themselves, the profession as a whole, and society at large are truly endless.

4. Jésus: "Esperar todo el dia y nada—nada para dar a la familia, nada para la renta, y nada para comer." ("You wait all day long, and nothing—nothing to send back to the family, nothing for rent, and nothing to eat.")

5. Gabriel: "He estudiado aqui. Hablo el Ingles. He intentado buscar trabajo en los hoteles, los restaurantes. Pero lo primero que quieren son los documentos." ("I studied here. I speak English. I've tried to find work in the hotels, the restaurants. But the first thing they want to see are your papers.")

6. Day Labor Station, 3-D diagram.

7. Day Labor Station, planometric.

4.

5.

Daily Operation

■ active = fluid: components allow varied uses
■ after hours = solid: contained box

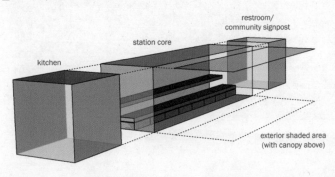

restroom/ community signpost

station core

kitchen

exterior shaded area (with canopy above)

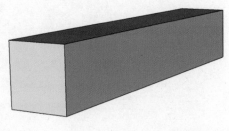

6.

active   after hours

Flexible Uses

□ interior seating area (built-in benches)
■ station service area
⬚ canopy above
■ pull-out bench

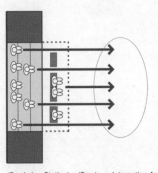

(Day Labor Station) (Employer Interaction Area)

"Employment Center"

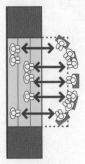

(Day Labor Station)

"Meeting Space"

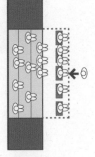

(Day Labor Station)

"Classroom"

7.

HEARING FOR ALL

Why was a solar-powered hearing-aid battery charger needed in Botswana?

MN: More than 278 million people worldwide have a disabling hearing impairment. Eighty percent of these people are based in developing countries, including Botswana and every other African country.

We found that many people with hearing disabilities do not continue in school, get involved in any economic activity, and so forth; and we have to intervene somewhere. We have to give people a tool, give them the ability to progress in schooling and in the workforce, something that won't keep them marginalized.

There are lots of hearing aids out there, but why are people not using them? Because they don't have the means to maintain them. A battery costs about anywhere from $5 to $12 and only lasts about seven days; but for people in poor countries, where they earn less than $5 a day, that is too costly. You're asking a parent to choose between a hearing aid and food; obviously, he or she will choose the more immediate need.

So we thought: We need to use a technology that is suitable for our areas, a technology that is affordable and cheaper. Why not have a rechargeable battery that will last from two to four years? We came up with this solution following some of the guidelines set out by the World Health Organization, and what the WHO wanted to see was a hearing aid that is affordable and which people will continue to use (fig.1).

Initially, we started with a body hearing aid, but deaf people everywhere prefer to not be conspicuous and have a big gadget on their bodies, so we took the conventional behind-the-ear hearing aid and used solar technology to recharge the battery.

Who was the designer of the Solar Aid recharger?

MN: This was a team effort. The designers of this recharger include our deaf employees and the management team during that year, and, of course, our board members have been very instrumental and have contributed a lot. We have hearing-aid specialists, an audiologist, and an engineer on our board, who used their specialized knowledge to guide us.

How has this affected the hearing-impaired in Botswana and other countries?

MN: This is certainly making an impact in that people are no longer putting the hearing aid aside after the battery runs low; they're recharging the battery and using it for longer. There's more consistent usage, and, of course, it's affordable. In generally developing countries like Botswana, people will travel up to one thousand kilometers to buy a $5 battery. They're spending more on the transport to buy this battery, which will last only up to about seven days, and then when they go back, what do they do? Come back again. The rechargeable batteries are saving people time and money.

INTERVIEW WITH
MODESTA NYIRENDA-ZABULA,
GODISA TECHNOLOGIES TRUST

BY CYNTHIA SMITH

1. Solar Aid solar battery recharger
with hearing aid and battery charging.

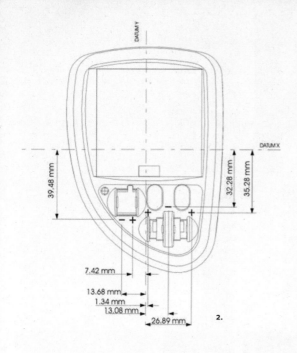

2.

Is it only in Botswana and other parts of Africa, or is it used in other places as well?

MN: We have our product in South and Central America, Africa, and Asia, and we're looking to reach as many developing countries as we can. We've recognized this is a priority need in developing countries; but there are also people in developed countries who need it, because batteries are expensive everywhere. Every person who uses a hearing aid has this problem.

So you're thinking you might bring this product to the developing world also? Where would your first location be? Do you have a plan for that?

MN: Yes, but we don't have a plan yet. We do know that we want to bring it to the United States and Europe. As for the first specific locations, we are working on it.

Where is the Solar Aid battery recharger manufactured?

MN: Botswana.

What is the cost of the recharger?

MN: The recharger itself costs about $20.00, $24.00 with the batteries.

How many are in use today?

MN: We have nearly 7,000 units in use today (fig.2).

Your organization has a unique makeup. Whom do you employ?

MN: Our organization's mission is to empower deaf people through employment, training, and education, and the first part of our mission is to make sure that people in developing countries receive high-quality hearing-care solutions at affordable prices. Because of our mission, we're focusing on employing people with hearing impairments. Currently,

ninety percent of our team is either deaf and/or physically disabled.

Tell us about yourself. How did you get involved with Godisa Technologies?

MN: In 1996, I moved from Zambia to join my parents, who were living in Botswana, and the first job I got after I arrived was for an organization, the Society for the Deaf, which ran two deaf schools. I worked and interacted with deaf and hearing-impaired people. I learned sign language, and learned about deaf culture. I began to understand the disability as well as the challenges of deaf people. After I worked there for about four years, my contract ended, and I decided to take a few months off. One of the deaf people I was counseling while working at the Society for the Deaf contacted me and told me about a project he wanted to start, and I was approached by the coordinator of the project at that time. Because of what I had already experienced, I was more than happy to get involved, and I joined Godisa Technologies Trust in 2002. We started as a two-person team, myself and a volunteer from Canada. His name was Howard Weinstein, and we worked together on the design of the charger. We recruited and trained about twenty deaf individuals, finally employing about ten. We eventually picked the best of those ten to be on the first Godisa team. What we've done annually since 2002 is to continue to train hearing-impaired people. We approach our local deaf school and ask for candidates who would like to join the team, or whom we can prepare for a job. It's not easy for a deaf person in Africa, definitely not in Botswana, to get a job straight out of school. So we bring them in and train them, then retain those who have the skills. If we feel there are other areas in which we can place hearing-impaired candidates, we help them get jobs elsewhere.

Do you plan on taking that model to other countries?

MN: It is in our future plans, yes. Definitely in developing countries; we're looking at either South America, the Middle East, or Pakistan, as they are areas in which we have partners taking the necessary steps toward such a model.

What is the connection between reducing poverty and creating this low-cost way to recharge batteries?

MN: In developing countries, healthcare systems need improvement. Most children born deaf, or people who become deaf, need intervention, and the best thing is to make sure that intervention happens at an early stage in order to integrate them as much as possible into society. They need to be taught how to be with everyone, how to live, how to not be marginalized and pushed to the side. What has happened in Africa and other developing countries is people with hearing disabilities are identified at a late stage, when they are ten years old, even going into their teens, and it is a very difficult problem to have. For example, a twelve-year-old child starting first grade has to be taught the basics of his own language, the alphabet, at that age.

2. Drawing and dimensions of the Solar Aid solar recharger.

3. Solar Aid solar recharger, hearing aid, and battery.

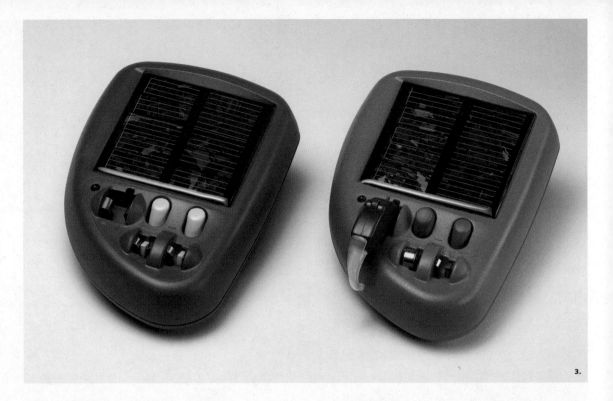

3.

And because of this delay, his life progress is also delayed, and this is what has brought a lot of poverty to people who are deaf or have a disabling hearing impairment. Hopefully, as our health systems improve, and we detect deafness earlier, we will encourage the continued use of hearing aids by making sure affordable solutions are available.

We know that we may not be able to afford top-range, high-tech hearing aids that may not even be necessarily suitable for our environment, but most of the developing countries are countries with plenty of sunshine. What better than solar technology for it? And batteries are very scarce. There's nothing better than making sure you're able to use your battery for the next three years. This is where the connection is.

And if you have someone who's born deaf and you give him the tools and enable that person, he is able to integrate better into society. He has a chance at education; he has a chance at employment; he has a chance to make a living.

Can you explain how one uses the batteries?

MN: You expose the charger's solar panel to sunlight. During the day, the solar panel captures power and stores it in reserve. You have two AA batteries in the back which work as reserve power. But even if you don't have the batteries in the back, you can still directly recharge the hearing aid. A hearing aid is retrofitted specifically for the charger (fig.3).

You can use your hearing aid all day, and when you come back at home at night, you just slot it in the charger, and it recharges overnight. And even if you don't have our hearing aid, if you still use a rechargeable battery, you can slot the battery in the battery slot. In the same way, it will get recharged overnight, and you're ready to go the next day.

POT-IN-POT COOLER

I grew up in a village in rural Nigeria. Most of the villages here are locked in the hinterlands. There is a problem of transportation, a lack of water, and don't forget, we are a developing nation. Therefore, these people have no electricity supply.

The biggest single problem for the farmers is the lack of preservation of their crops. The climate here is too harsh. This is a very dry region.

The earthen pot is an indigenous traditional technology. I know it cools. You can use it just to store drinking water, but, I wondered, can it be used for other things as well? Then I started making advancements with the pot.

The pot-in-pot system consists of two pots, a bigger outer pot and a small inner one. Now, the farmer is required to put fine, wet sand in between the smaller inner pot and the bigger outer pot and to protect and keep it moist (fig. 1). Something like spinach can last for days in this manner, as opposed to only one or two days under normal circumstances (fig. 2). Tomatoes last for twenty-one days, as opposed to two or three days under normal circumstances.

When I discovered that the system worked well, I single-handedly financed the first 5,000 pot-in-pot systems for my municipality as well as in five other villages (fig. 3). I feel excited, as this will revolutionize life in the rural areas.

These girls are from Goromo Village. They are now on their way to the market to sell mangos and all the other perishable items (fig. 4). Now, these are the kind of girls I am trying to deliver the system to. For these girls, going to school used to be out of the question. Now, all of these items can be preserved at home in the pots and sold on demand, and they can be free to go back to school (fig. 5).

The pot-in-pot system doesn't require electricity. The raw materials needed to manufacture the pots are not only acquired nationally, but they are, of course, free for a country like Nigeria, which has more than 114 million people. The government cannot be the supplier of everything. People have to be self-reliant. The pot-in-pot system is an initiative that is helping the lives of these people.

MOHAMMED BAH ABBA

TAKEN FROM A FILM
COURTESY OF ROLEX AWARDS
FOR ENTERPRISE

1. Pot-in-pot at the market in Dutse, Nigeria.

2. Onions preserved with the Pot-in-Pot at the market in Dutse, Nigeria.

3. Market in Dutse, Nigeria, one of the few places where earthen pots are sold for everyday use.

4. Girls from the village of Goromo, Nigeria, hawking food.

5. Aisha Salah writing lessons at the Sumore primary school, Nigeria.

6. Earthen pots were used traditionally in the area, but have fallen out of use.

2.

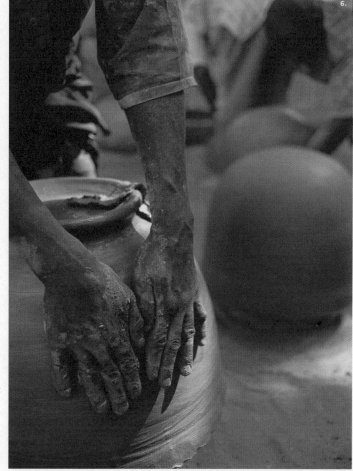

EXHIBITION OBJECTS

AMD PERSONAL INTERNET COMMUNICATOR

DESIGNER: M3 Design

MANUFACTURER: Solectron and FIC
United States, Mexico, and Brazil, 2004
Cast aluminum base, molded PC/ABS plastic two-piece external shell finished, TPE trim band, rubber feet; 10GB 3.5 internal hard disk running on an AMD Geode™ GX processor, screws

DIMENSIONS: 2.5 h x 5.5 w x 8.5 d

USED IN: Brazil, British Virgin Islands, India, Jamaica, Mexico, Panama, Russia, South Africa, Turkey, Uganda, United States

COURTESY OF M3 DESIGN

Currently, less than 15% of the world's population has access to the Internet. AMD's Personal Internet Communicator was designed specifically to provide basic computing functionality, including Internet access, at affordable prices. AMD's 50x15 initiative is an effort to develop new technology and solutions that will help enable affordable Internet access and computing capability for 50 percent of the world's population by the year 2015.

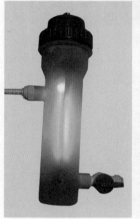

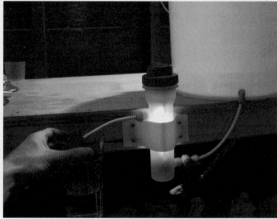

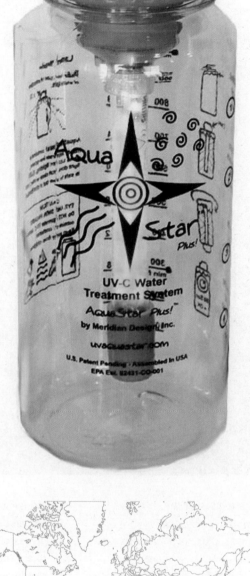

AQUASTAR PLUS! AND FLOW THROUGH

DESIGNER/MANUFACTURER:
Meridian Design
United States, 2005 and 2006
(Plus) Quartz glass, argon gas, low-pressure mercury vapor (UVC germicidal lamp), ABS plastic, polycarbonate plastic bottle (body), fiberglass and epoxy resin circuit components, silicon, plastic, tinned plated copper leads (circuit board), lithium batteries; (Flow Through) ABS plastic
DIMENSIONS: (Plus) 9 h x 4 diameter; (Flow Through) 4 h x 4 w x 10 d
USED IN: Australia, Borneo, Guatemala, India, Malaysia, Mexico, New Zealand, Nicaragua, Peru

AquaStar was designed to be sold to a high-end market to fund a lower-cost application in the developing world. The more expensive AquaStar Plus! is used in the harshest environments by travelers, military personnel, and rescue workers. Unsafe water is placed in the bottle and exposed to UV-C light, which damages the DNA and RNA in the pathogens, rendering them non-infective. AquaStar Flow Through treats water in larger batches. A small water-purification service can generate income while helping out the community.

One in five children—nearly 400 million—has no access to safe water.

BAMBOO TREADLE PUMP

DESIGNER: Gunnar Barnes of
Rangpur/Dinajpur Rural Service and
International Development Enterprises
(IDE) Nepal

MANUFACTURER: Numerous small
and medium-sized local workshops
Nepal and Bangladesh, 2006
Metal, plastic, bamboo

DIMENSIONS: 5′ h x 2.5′ w x 7′ d

USED IN: Bangladesh, Cambodia, India,
Myanmar, Nepal, Zambia

COURTESY OF PAUL POLAK, IDE

The Bamboo Treadle Pump allows poor
farmers to access groundwater during the
dry season. The treadles and support structure are made of bamboo or other inexpensive, locally available materials. The pump,
which consists of two metal cylinders with
pistons operated by a natural walking mo-
tion on two treadles, can be manufactured
locally by metalworking shops. More than
1.7 million have been sold in Bangladesh
and elsewhere, generating $1.4 billion in net
farmer income in Bangladesh alone.

More than 840 million people in the world are malnourished, of
which 799 million live in the developing world.

BIG BODA LOAD-CARRYING BICYCLE

DESIGNERS: WorldBike, Adam French (first phase), Ed Lucero, with contributions from Paul Freedman, Matt Snyder, Ross Evans, Moses Odhiambo, and Jacob (second phase)

MANUFACTURER: WorldBike and Moses Odhiambo's workshop

Kenya, 2002–05

Mild steel, woven papyrus passenger cushion

DIMENSIONS: 84 h x 48 w x 24 d

USED IN: Kenya, Uganda

COURTESY OF WORLDBIKE

The Big Boda is able to carry hundreds of pounds of cargo or two additional passengers easily, at a substantially lower cost than other forms of human-powered utility vehicles. It was designed to transport goods to and from market for entrepreneurs and consumers in developing countries. WorldBike originally designed a low-cost frame extension called the Longtail to be compatible with the low-cost Chinese-made single-speeds ubiquitous in East Africa. In 2005, it was redesigned to be more suitable with the Western Kenyan Boda Boda bicycle-taxi operators and for easier manufacturing in small workshops.

CERAMIC WATER FILTER, CAMBODIA

DESIGNERS: Dr. Fernando Mazariegos,
Ron Rivera (Potters for Peace), and
International Development Enterprises
(IDE) Cambodia

MANUFACTURER: Local private factory
set up by IDE
Cambodia, 2006
Ceramic clay, plastic container,
colloidal silver paint

DIMENSIONS: 3.5´ h x 2´ w x 2´ d

COURTESY OF PAUL POLAK, IDE

CERAMIC WATER FILTER, NEPAL

DESIGNER: Deepak Adhikari, IDE, and
Reid Harvey, consultant

MANUFACTURER: Local potter set
up by IDE
Nepal, 2006
Ceramic clay, plastic container,
colloidal silver paint

DIMENSIONS: 3.5´ h x 2´ w x 2´ d

COURTESY OF PAUL POLAK, IDE

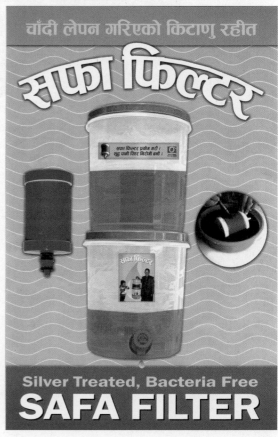

चांदी लेपन गरिएको किटाणु रहीत

सफा फिल्टर

Silver Treated, Bacteria Free
SAFA FILTER

CERAMIC WATER FILTER, NICARAGUA

Designers: Dr. Fernando Mazariegos
and Ron Rivera (Potters for Peace)
MANUFACTURER: Filtron
Nicaragua and Guatemala, 2006
Local Nicaraguan terra-cotta clay,
sawdust
DIMENSIONS: 18 h x 15 diameter
COURTESY OF POTTERS FOR PEACE

USED IN: Cambodia, Cuba, Ghana,
Guatemala, Ecuador, El Salvador, Haiti,
Honduras, India, Indonesia (Bali), Iraq,
Mexico, Myanmar, Nepal, Nicaragua,
Sudan, Thailand, Vietnam

Originally designed by Dr. Fernando
Mazareigos, a Guatemalan chemist, the
Ceramic Water Filter combines the filtra-
tion capability of ceramic material with the
anti-bacteriological qualities of colloidal
silver. This filter has basic, yet impressive,
impact on the lives of the rural poor, dramatically decreasing diarrhea, days of
school or work missed due to illness, and
medical expenses. A sociologist and potter,
Ron Rivera of Potters for Peace redesigned
the filter to standardize mass production
in sixteen small production facilities in fourteen different countries. It is estimated
that more than 500,000 people have used
the filter.

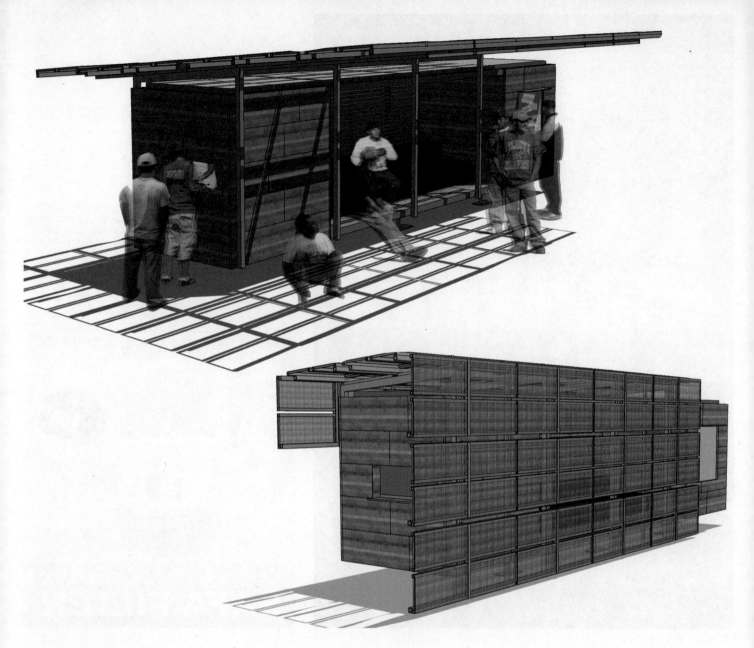

DAY LABOR STATION

PROJECT TEAM: Public Architecture:
John Peterson, Design Director; Liz Ogbu,
Designer/Project Manager

CONSTRUCTION PROJECT PARTNER:
Ryan Construction
United States, 2006–07
Wood, metal
Dimensions: 12' h x 8' w x 10' d, 9' canopy

USED IN: United States

COURTESY OF PUBLIC ARCHITECTURE AND RYAN CONSTRUCTION
THANKS TO: ANOTONIO, GABRIEL, JESUS, LEOBARDO, ROBERTO
(DAY LABORERS); JOHN CARY, EXECUTIVE DIRECTOR, AND DEB
GRANT, DIRECTOR OF DEVELOPMENT, PUBLIC ARCHITECTURE;
RYAN ASSOCIATES; ELENA DORFMAN PHOTOGRAPHY; KIRK WUEST;
MENDEDESIGN; REDCLAY; ROBYN COLOR; SIMON & ASSOCIATES;
SINTAK STUDIO; SYD ELKINS; MATT ENERING; MICHELLE HUBER;
KIEL SCHMIDT; TAYLOR WRIGHT

An estimated 117,000 day laborers look for
work each day in the United States, working in an informal economy. The Day Labor
Station accommodates waiting day laborers, organizational meetings, classes, and
sanitation facilities, without requiring staff.
The mobile center unit is designed to be
built by day laborers themselves and deployed at informal hiring sites. Local organizations are given the opportunity to
schedule on-site classes, including English
as a second language, legal assistance, and
civil-rights workshops.

DOMED PIT LATRINE SLAB KIT

DESIGNER: Martin Fisher
MANUFACTURER: KickStart International
Kenya, 1992
Mild steel, local hard wood (kits); sand,
cement, gravel, ballast, wire (slabs)
DIMENSIONS: 5.5′ x 5.5′
USED IN: Ethiopia, Kenya, Somalia, Sudan
COURTESY OF KICKSTART INTERNATIONAL

The KickStart Domed Pit Latrine Slab
design is based on a concept of a latrine
slab by Bjorn Brandberg at the National
Institute of Physical Planning in
Mozambique. KickStart redesigned the
production methods to allow for simple,
high-quality mass production of the slabs
working with unskilled local laborers; and
improved the overall design for better sanitation and lower cost. The dome shape
minimizes the required thickness, making it
cheaper than typical reinforced concrete
slabs; a tight fitting lid creates a tight seal
to keep the smell in and the flies out; and
the wire handle heats up from sunlight,
killing germs and reducing contamination.
They are the standard in refugee camps in
East Africa, where more than 90,000 slabs
have now been installed.

Nearly two billion people live without access to basic sanitation.

DRIP IRRIGATION SYSTEM

DESIGNER: International Development Enterprises (IDE) India
MANUFACTURER: Multiple workshops
India, 2006
Plastic tubing and tank
DIMENSIONS: 2′ h x 2′ w x 8 d (with water); bag can hang from any type of post or support and tailored to any size or shape available
USED IN: India, Nepal, Zambia, Zimbabwe

COURTESY OF PAUL POLAK, IDE

IDE's low-cost Drip Irrigation System was developed so farmers could start small and scale up as their financial capacity and acreage grew. The kits are significantly less expensive than conventional drip systems used on commercial farms. Studies show that drip irrigation reduces water use by 30-70% and increases yields by more than 50%. There is improved crop quality, crop-per-drop efficiency for agricultural intensification, and cultivation of high-value marketable crops. The kits, operating under very little water pressure, are typically used in the production of fruit and vegetable crops, but have also been used for maize, wheat, and cotton. More than 600,000 systems have been sold.

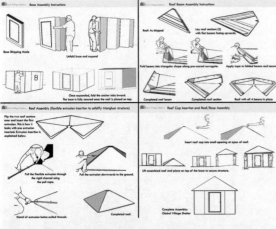

GLOBAL VILLAGE SHELTER

DESIGNER: Ferrara Design, Inc.,
with Architecture for Humanity

MANUFACTURER: Weyerhauser Company
United States, 2004
Triple wall-laminated corrugated card-
board treated with fire-resistant and
waterproof coating, thermoformed
general purpose ABS

DIMENSIONS: 92 h x 98.5 w x 98.5 d

USED IN: Afghanistan, Grenada, Pakistan,
southern Asia, United States

COURTESY OF GLOBAL VILLAGE SHELTERS, LLC

Global Village Shelters, made from
biodegradable laminated material, are
low-cost temporary emergency shelters
that can last up to eighteen months.
Prefabricated, shipped flat, and requiring
no tools to assemble, they are easy to de-
ploy. The first prototypes were sent to
Afghanistan and Grenada, and later used in
tsunami-hit countries in Asia; Pakistan's
Azad Kashmir Province, which was devastated by an earthquake; and to Gulfport,
Mississippi, after Hurricane Katrina.

There are currently twenty-one million internally displaced persons, in addition to
twelve million refugees and asylum seekers, needing temporary shelter.

In 2001, 2.7 billion people internationally were living on less than $2 a day.

HOUSE OF DANCE & FEATHERS

FOUNDER: Ronald Lewis

DESIGN/MANUFACTURING TEAM: Project Locus, Larry Bowne, Caitlin Heckathorn; student volunteers from Kansas State University, IIT, and University of California, Berkeley

PROJECT PARTNERS: Tulane City Center, Tulane University; University of Montana Department of Environmental Studies; CITYBuild; Common Ground

DONORS: Charles Engelhart Foundation, Barry M. Downing Foundation, Lucite International, Flavor Paper, Lighting Inc., General Electric, LJ Goldstein, Grainger, Linweld, National Polyfab, Sherwin Williams New Orleans, Palram

United States, 2006

Poured-in-place concrete, rebar, concrete block, treated lumber and decking, prefabricated steel plates and moment connections, plywood subfloor, galvanized steel wire cable, stainless-steel turnbuckles, recycled galvanized metal roofing, clear polycarbonate roof panels, CP acrylic panels, ¾ cabinet-grade maple plywood, wood stain, recycled antique door, recycled bolts and aluminum entry doors, custom commercial EMT conduit and wiring, commercial junction boxes, outlets, switches and cover plates, custom screen-printed and polyurethaned paper flooring, recycled screen-print frames, exhibit panels, stainless-steel-coated peg board, in-

terior lighting, RAB Vapor exterior lighting, Minka ceiling fans

DIMENSIONS: 12′ x 32′, 384 square feet

GATEKEEPER STAFF

DESIGNER: Unknown

MANUFACTURER: Unknown

United States, date unknown

Wood, metal, faux fur, bells, ribbon, Styrofoam

DIMENSIONS: 68 h x 5 w

COURTESY OF RONALD LEWIS

Ronald Lewis's House of Dance and Feathers celebrates the Big Nine Social Aid and Pleasure Club, the oldest such club in the Ninth Ward, and Mardi Gras Indian tribes throughout New Orleans. Project Locus rebuilt the backyard museum to help reconstruct a sense of history and identity for this unique culture after Hurricane Katrina destroyed the original location. The hardest-hit victims of this tragedy were the poor and disadvantaged living in the center of the city, who lacked the means to escape. More than 100,000 homes were lost in New Orleans alone. The museum, a flagship of the devastated Lower Ninth Ward, was rebuilt as a practical and cultural design resource for members of the community. The staff, a gift from a Creole Wild West member, now protects the site.

INTERNET VILLAGE MOTOMAN

NETWORK
American Assistance for Cambodia, Operation Village Heath, Sihanouk Hospital Center of Hope, Massachusetts General Hospital/Harvard Medical School

MOBILE ACCESS POINT AND ANTENNA
DESIGNER/MANUFACTURER:
United Villages, Inc.
antenna by HyperLink Technologies, Inc., United States, 2002–03
DIMENSIONS: 6 h x 12 w x 4 d (box), 15 (antenna)
COURTESY OF AMIR ALEXANDER HASSAN

SOLAR PANEL
MANUFACTURER: Kyocera Corporation
Japan, 2006
DIMENSIONS: 40 h x 25.5 w x 2.5 d
COURTESY OF KYOCERA CORPORATION

IPSTAR BROADBAND SATELLITE SYSTEM
MANUFACTURER: Shin Satellite Plc.
DIMENSIONS: 33 diameter
COURTESY OF SHIN SATELLITE PLC. OF THAILAND

HELMET
MANUFACTURER: S.Y.K. Autopart Import-Export Co., Ltd.
Thailand, date unknown
ABS plastic
DIMENSIONS: 9.5 h x 10.2 w x 23.6 l
COURTESY OF AMERICAN ASSISTANCE FOR CAMBODIA

MOTORCYCLE
DESIGNER/MANUFACTURER:
Honda Motor Co., Ltd.
Thailand, 2002
DIMENSIONS: 41.3 h x 27.5 w x 73.5 l
COURTESY OF HONDA MOTOR CO., LTD.

USED IN: Cambodia, Costa Rica, India, Paraguay, Rwanda

The Internet Village Motoman was launched for fifteen solar-powered village schools, telemedicine clinics, and the governor's office in Ratanakiri, a remote province of Cambodia, using five Honda motorcycles equipped with mobile access points and a satellite uplink. Each of the schools can send and receive email and browse the Internet using a non-real-time search engine. The network was implemented for American Assistance for Cambodia, which operates more than 200 rural schools. Telemedicine clinics, held in remote areas of Cambodia by Operation Village Health, give patients access to physicians in Boston, Massachusetts. A visiting nurse from Phnom Penh makes the six-hour trip by truck to each village to interview, examine, and digitally photograph patients, then transmits the information by satellite to physicians in Boston using a solar-powered computer. Within hours, the physicians respond with medical opinions and treatment recommendations.

Less than 15% of the world's total population has
Internet access.

KATRINA FURNITURE PROJECT

DESIGNER/MANUFACTURER:
University of Texas and Art Center College
of Design students and faculty
United States, 2006
Wood recycled from
Hurricane Katrina debris
DIMENSIONS: 32 h x 72 w (pew);
17 h x 18 w x 8 d, 20 h x 9 w x 10 d,
20 h x 7½ w x 10 d (step stools);
29 h x 34 w x 72 d (table)
USED IN: United States

COURTESY OF SERGIO PALLERONI AND
BASIC INITIATIVE, UNIVERSITY OF TEXAS

In 2001, 1.1 billion people were living on less than the international poverty
line set by the World Bank at the relative equivalent of $1 per day.

Hurricane Katrina left an estimated 1.5 million Americans homeless along the Gulf Coast region.

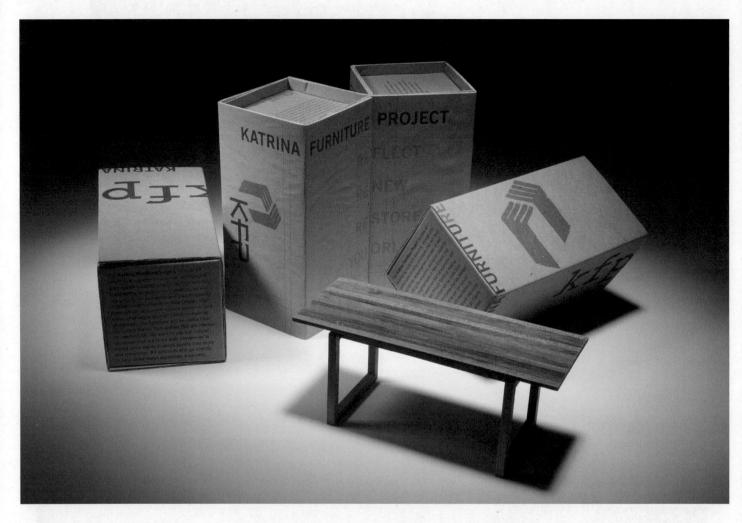

YOUORLEANS

DESIGNERS: Graphic Design department, Art Center College of Design; alumni Jae Chae, Ayumi Ito, Atley Kasky; students John Emshwiller, Janet Ferrero, Matthew Potter; project director and department chair Nik Hafermaas; lead instructor Paul Hauge; in collaboration with the Designmatters initiative
United States, 2006–07
Recycled cypress, recycled e-flute material, recycled paper stock
USED IN: United States

The Katrina Furniture Project, formed in response to Hurricane Katrina, creates neighborhood furniture-making workshop facilities using the debris left by the storm and helps build the economic and social capacity of neighborhoods in New Orleans, especially those that faced severe economic and social challenges even before Katrina. The workshops train community members in making furniture and the fundamentals of business, and function as a neighborhood-based place of work and resource center while residents rebuild their homes. Workshops will make and sell church pews—to replace those lost to the more than ninety churches ruined by the storm—as well as tables and stools, all from recycled wood.

YouOrleans is an identity system developed by a team of students, alumni, and instructors from Art Center College of Design, formed to brand the Katrina Furniture Project. The identity graphically represents the resilient and ever-optimistic citizens of New Orleans as well the craftspeople at the Katrina Furniture Project, who are using their talent and determination to effect recovery and reclaim their lives. In collaboration with Art Center's Designmatters initiative, a United Nations–designated non-governmental organization (NGO) which acts as an educational laboratory for best practices and social engagement, the project based its design solution on the typographic identifier of "Re"—as in Recovery, Revitalization, Reformation, Reuse, Redevelop, and Redeem—embodied in the furniture.

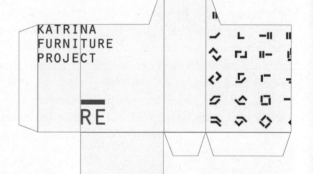

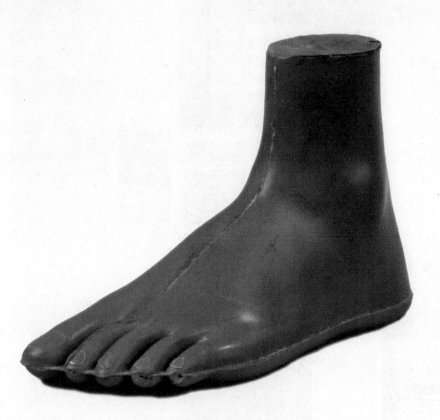

JAIPUR FOOT AND BELOW-KNEE PROSTHESIS

DESIGNERS: Master Ram Chandra Sharma and Dr P. K. Sethi

MANUFACTURER: Bhagwan Mahavir Viklang Sahayata Samiti
Jaipur, India, 1968
Micro-cellular rubber, cosmetic rubber compound, nylon cord rubber, trade rubber compound, cushion rubber compound, wooden keel with a connection bolt (foot); HDPE (high-density polyethylene) pipe and sheet, Jaipur foot, padeline sheet, leather straps (below-knee)

DIMENSIONS: 9.5 (foot), 9 (instep), 9 (ball girth), 21 (below-knee), 19.5 (maximum diameter)

USED IN: Afghanisthan, Bangladesh, Dominican Republic, Honduras, Indonesia, Malawi, Nigeria, Nepal, Nairobi, Panama, Philippines, Papua New Guinea, Rwanda, Somalia, Sudan, Trinidad, Vietnam, Zimbabwe

COURTESY OF BHAGWAN MAHAVIR VIKLANG
SAHAYATA SAMITI

The Jaipur prosthesis is low-cost, durable, waterproof, and can be used with or without shoes. Ram Chandra Sharma, a craftsman, and Dr P. K. Sethi, an orthopedic surgeon, designed this improved version of a conventional prosthetic foot. The Jaipur foot, named for the town where it was designed, is flexible along multiple axes, which allows natural movement of the foot. The Jaipur foot technology is based on traditional craft using small local production methods, and has already helped more than 900,000 amputees in developing and landmine-affected countries.

At least 1.3 billion people worldwide lack access to the most basic healthcare.

KENYA CERAMIC JIKO

DESIGNERS: International aid and governmental agencies, local women's organizations, and craftspeople

MANUFACTURER: Rural Technology Enterprises

Kenya, 1982–83

Ceramic lining, metal rings

DIMENSIONS: 6 h x 9.5 diameter (small), 7 h x 11 diameter (standard), 9 h x 12 diameter (medium), 11.5 h x 15 diameter (large), 14 h x 17 diameter (extra large)

USED IN: Burundi, Democratic Republic of Congo, Ethiopia, Kenya, Malawi, Niger, Rwanda, Senegal, Sudan, Tanzania, Uganda

COURTESY OF KICKSTART INTERNATIONAL

The Kenya Ceramic Jiko is a portable charcoal stove which, with proper use and maintenance, can reduce fuel consumption by 30-50%, saving the consumer money, reducing toxic gas and particulate matter, and resulting in better overall health for the user. The stove is now used in more than 50% of all urban homes and 16% of rural homes in Kenya and is spreading to neighboring African countries.

Wood energy remains the most important source of energy for two billion people in developing countries who have little access to other sources of energy.

KINKAJOU MICROFILM PROJECTOR + PORTABLE LIBRARY

DESIGNERS: Design that Matters, Inc., in collaboration with students and professionals

MANUFACTURER: Various contract manufacturers in the New England area United States, 2004

6061-T6 and 6063 aluminum, ABS plastic, polycarbonate or PMMA lenses, acetyl plastic lens barrels, stainless steel screws, glass-epoxy composite circuit board

DIMENSIONS: 11 h x 7 w x 3 d (projector), 19.5 h x 15 w x 1 d (solar panel), 10 h x 8.5 w x 3.5 d (battery pack)

USED IN: Mali; Bangladesh, Benin, India (field tests)

COURTESY OF DESIGN THAT MATTERS, INC.

The Kinkajou Projector is a low-cost teaching tool designed to improve and expand access to education by transforming nighttime learning environments in rural, non-electrified areas. The project's mission is to improve adult literacy in rural West Africa, where up to 75% of the adult population is illiterate. Eliminating the need for books, which are expensive and difficult to distribute in places where adult classes are held at night by oil lamps, Kinkajou combines the efficiency of LEDs with the durability and storage capacity of microfilm. The unit is easy to maintain and includes a solar panel for off-grid use. Kinkajou's primary beneficiaries are the most disadvantaged and hardest to reach individuals: poor, rural women. Literacy contributes decisively to improving a community's quality of life through improved health and child nutrition. Kinkajou projectors have helped more than 3,000 adults in forty-five rural villages in Mali learn to read.

Eight hundred fifty-five million people worldwide are illiterate. Of that number, two-thirds are women.

LIFESTRAW

DESIGNER: Vestergaard Frandsen
MANUFACTURER: Vestergaard Frandsen s.a.
China and Switzerland, 2005
(current version)
High impact polystyrene (outer shell),
halogen-based resin, anion exchange
resin, and patented activated
carbon (interior)
DIMENSIONS: 10 h x 1 diameter
USED IN: Ghana, Nigeria, Pakistan, Uganda

COURTESY OF VESTERGAARD FRANDSEN S.A.

About half of the world's poor suffer from
waterborne diseases, and more than 6,000
people, mainly children, die each day by
consuming unsafe drinking water.
LifeStraw, a personal mobile water-purification tool, is designed to turn any surface
water into drinking water. It has proven
to be effective against waterborne diseases
such as typhoid, cholera, dysentery, and
diarrhea, and removes particles as small
as fifteen microns.

Waterborne diseases are estimated to cause more
than two million deaths annually.

MAD HOUSERS HUT

DESIGNER/MANUFACTURER: Mad Housers volunteers
United States, 1987
Lumber (1x6 and 2x4 studs), plywood ($\frac{3}{8}$ and $\frac{5}{8}$), nails (16 penny, 8 penny, finishing, roofing), roll roofing, plastic and/or screen for windows, silver sheet insulation, paint, caulk, metal flashing, stove pipe, cinderblocks, stove, 55-gallon steel drum
DIMENSIONS: 10′ h x 6′ w x 8′ d
USED IN: Canada, United States

COURTESY OF MAD HOUSERS

Mad Housers was started by a small group of Georgia Tech architecture students in 1987 with a mission of building free shelter for Atlanta's homeless. Each hut has a locking door for security, a loft for sleeping and storage, and a wood-burning stove for cooking and heat. The prefabricated huts can be erected in less than half a day. Huts are built in stable sites where a client has camped for some time and is not likely to be torn down, and, in some cases, where the landowners give permission for them to be built. The huts are not intended as permanent housing, but rather as temporary shelters, with the idea that people with a secure and stable place to live are much more capable of finding other resources to help themselves.

In the United States, approximately 3.5 million people experience homelessness each year.

MONEYMAKER BLOCK PRESS

DESIGNER: Martin Fisher

MANUFACTURER: KickStart International
Kenya, 1986

100% mild steel

DIMENSIONS: 39.5 h x 20 w x 20 d (base
unit), 79 h x 16 w x 8 d (handle)

USED IN: Democratic Republic of Congo,
Kenya, Malawi, Rwanda, Somalia, Sudan,
Tanzania, Uganda, Zambia

COURTESY OF KICKSTART INTERNATIONAL

More than 2,200 KickStart MoneyMaker
Block Presses have been sold to East
African block-making and construction
businesses to build cost-effective homes,

schools, and commercial buildings. The
press makes strong and durable building
blocks from soil mixed with a small percentage of cement, compressed at high
pressure and cured for ten days. The press
accommodates operators of different sizes
and strength, allows for high-compaction
blocks, and includes a built-in variable
volume batch box to allow for different
types of soils, with the resultant block
always having maximum density and
standard dimensions. Five to eight workers
can produce 400 to 800 blocks a day using
the press.

MONEYMAKER HIP PUMP

Designers: Martin Fisher, Alan Spybey,
Mohamed Swaleh, and Frederick Obudho
MANUFACTURER: KickStart International
Kenya and China, 2005
Mild steel, PVC, HDPE
DIMENSIONS: 32 h x 14 w x 27 d
USED IN: Kenya, Mali, Tanzania

COURTESY OF KICKSTART INTERNATIONAL

The MoneyMaker Hip Pump, launched in
2006, is a lightweight, easy-to-use pressure
pump that can irrigate three-quarters of
an acre over an eight-hour period, pulling
water from a depth of six meters and lifting
it to a height of thirteen meters above the
water source. In the first ten months, more
than 1,400 units have been bought by fledg-
ling family farming businesses. On average,
users of the Hip Pump have increased
their net farm income by over $125, tripling
their initial investment of $34 after three
or four months.

ONE LAPTOP PER CHILD

CONCEPT: Nicholas Negroponte
DESIGNER: Yves Béhar, fuseproject
(with Martin Schnitzer and Bret Recor),
Continuum (prototype), Human power:
Squid Labs (engineering)
SOFTWARE: Red Hat
PROCESSOR: Advanced Micro Devices
MANUFACTURER: Quanta Computer, Inc.,
and OLPC
China, 2007
PC/ABS, rubber
DIMENSIONS: 1.5 h x 9 w x 9.5 d
EXPECTED LAUNCH COUNTRIES: Argentina,
Brazil, Libya, Nigeria, Thailand, Uruguay
SECOND-WAVE LAUNCH COUNTRIES: Angola,
Belize, Costa Rica, Democratic Republic of
Congo, El Salvador, Ethiopia, Guatemala,
Honduras, Indonesia, Nicaragua,
Pakistan, Panama, Philippines, Vietnam

COURTESY OF YVÉS BEHAR, FUSEPROJECT

The One Laptop per Child, or $100 laptop, is a laptop computer designed as an educational tool to bring learning, information, and communication to children in developing countries. OLPC is a new experiment in socially responsible design, in which a nonprofit organization harnesses cutting-edge personal technologies and distributes them on an unprecedented scale. Governments purchase the laptops directly and distribute them to their schools.

One hundred twenty-one million children worldwide are not enrolled in primary school. The majority of them are girls.

PERMANET

DESIGNER: Vestergaard Frandsen
MANUFACTURER: Vestergaard Frandsen S.A.
Switzerland and Vietnam, 2000
100% polyester impregnated with
deltamethrin (synthetic parathyroid)
DIMENSIONS: 63 h x 71 w x 59 d
USED IN: Angola, Bangladesh, Benin,
Bhutan, Bolivia, Botswana, Burkina Faso,
Burundi, Cambodia, Cameroon, Central
African Republic, Chad, China, Côte
d'Ivoire, Democratic Republic of Congo,
Djibouti, Ecuador, Equatorial Guinea,
Eritrea, Ethiopia, French Guyana, Gabon,
Gambia, Ghana, Guatemala, Guinea,
Guinea-Bissau, Haiti, India, Indonesia,
Kenya, Laos, Lesotho, Liberia, Malawi,

About 90% of malaria deaths occur in sub-Saharan Africa, where one million people,
most of them children under five, die each year from the disease

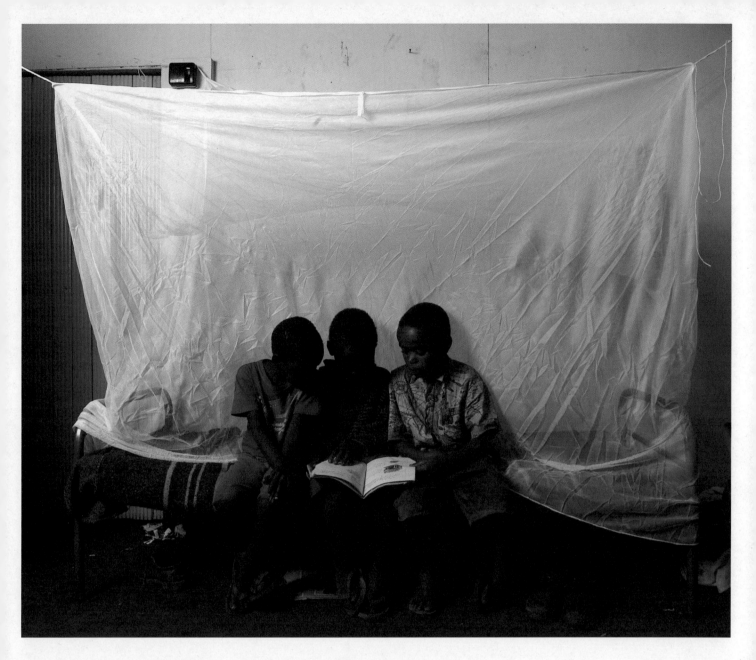

Malaysia, Mali, Mauritania, Mozambique, Myanmar, Namibia, Nepal, Nicaragua, Niger, Nigeria, North Korea, Papua New Guinea, Philippines, Republic of Congo, Rwanda, Senegal, Sierra Leone, Somalia, South Africa, Sri Lanka, Swaziland, Sudan, Suriname, Tanzania, Togo, Thailand, Uganda, Venezuela, Vietnam, West Pacific, Zambia, Zimbabwe,

COURTESY OF VESTERGAARD FRANDSEN S.A.

PermaNet is a long-lasting, insecticide-treated mosquito net commonly used in Africa by people who live among malarial mosquitoes. The net kills or repels mosquitoes for up to four years—five times longer than other treated nets—without losing effectiveness, even after twenty washes. Low re-treatment rates represent the biggest challenge in the fight against malaria, the infectious disease that kills more children than any other illness in Africa. Malaria kills millions each year, helping to make economic growth in countries with high malaria transmission historically lower than in countries without malaria.

POT-IN-POT COOLER

DESIGNER: Mohammed Bah Abba
MANUFACTURER: local potters
Nigeria, 1995
Earthenware, sand, water
DIMENSIONS: 16 to 22 diameter
USED IN: Burkina Faso, Cameroon, Chad, Eritrea, Ethiopia, Niger

COURTESY OF MOHAMMED BAH ABBA

The pot-in-pot system consists of a smaller earthenware pot nestled within another pot, with the space in between filled with sand and water. When that water evaporates, it pulls heat from the interior of the smaller pot, in which vegetables and fruits can be kept. In rural Nigeria, many farmers lack transportation, water, and electricity, but one of their biggest problems is the inability to preserve their crops. With the pot-in-pot, tomatoes last for twenty-one days, rather than two or three days without this technology. Fresher produce can be sold at the market, generating more income for the farmers.

Q DRUM

DESIGNER: P. J. and J. P. S. Hendrikse
MANUFACTURER: Kaymac Rotomoulders
and Pioneer Plastics
South Africa, 1993
Linear Low Density Polyethelene (LLDPE)
DIMENSIONS: 14 h x 19.5 diameter
USED IN: Angola, Côte d'Ivoire, Ethiopia,
Ghana, Kenya, Namibia, Nigeria, Rwanda,
South Africa, Tanzania

COURTESY OF P. J. HENDRIKSE

Millions around the world, especially in rural Africa, live kilometers from a reliable source of clean water, leaving them vulnerable to cholera, dysentery, and other water-borne diseases. Water in adequate quantities is too heavy to carry. The Q Drum is a durable container designed to roll easily and transport seventy-five liters of clean and potable water. Rolling the water in a cylindrical container, rather than lifting and carrying it, eases the burden of bringing water to those who need it.

Each day, 3,900 children die because they lack access to safe drinking water and adequate sanitation.

SEVENTH WARD SHADE PAVILION

CLIENT: The Porch Community Center

DESIGN/MANUFACTURING TEAM:
University of Kansas School of
Architecture and Urban Design
United States, 2006
Laminated ¾ plywood cut by CNC router,
mortise and tenon joints, custom steel
hardware for hurricane clips, base plates

DIMENSIONS: 12′ h x 12′ w x 16′ d (module)

USED IN: United States

COURTESY OF UNIVERSITY OF KANSAS SCHOOL OF ARCHITECTURE & URBAN DESIGN, ROB CORSER, AIA

The Seventh Ward Shade Pavilion provides
a temporary gathering and socializing place
while a permanent home is being
constructed for the Porch Community
Center, an organization committed to
sustaining the multitude of cultures in New
Orleans. Although located in a garden, the
resource center serves its originally
imagined function of providing rebuilding
assistance through access to tools,
information, and instruction in building
repair. It also serves as a site for classes in
gardening and as a new, highly visible
location for neighborhood gatherings of all
kinds. Intelligent construction systems are
developed for prefabrication in Kansas and
deployed in New Orleans as complete
sections, and can be expanded upon.

*assemble
frame*

*apply
cladding*

tilt - up

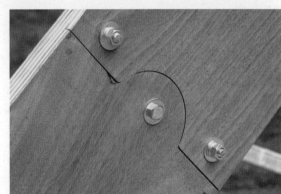

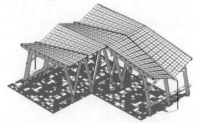

expansion & variation

SIERRA PORTABLE LIGHT PROTOTYPES

PORTABLE LIGHT MAT AND WORKSHOP LANTERN

CONCEPT, TEXTILE DESIGN, TECHNOLOGY
DEVELOPMENT: KVA and Patricia Gruits,
Sheila Kennedy, Sloan Kulper, Jason
O'Mara, Casey Smith, and Heather
Micka-Smith, Portable Light Design
Team; Dr. Stacy Schaefer, California State
University, Chico
United States, 2006
Woven aluminum textile, recyclable PET,
flexible photovoltaics, semiconductors,
flexible wireways
DIMENSIONS: 28 h x 14 w x 1 d (unfolded),
12 h x 14 w x 1 d (folded)

TRADITIONAL INTEGRATED PORTABLE
LIGHT TEXTILES

LIGHT KIT CONCEPT AND TECHNOLOGY:
KVA; Huichol bag and woven portable light
kits: Estella Hernandez and family
United States and Mexico, 2006
Acrylic yarn or natural wool, flexible semi-
conductor technologies
DIMENSIONS: 8 h x 6 w x .5 d
USED IN: Australia, Mexico (pilot programs)

COURTESY OF KENNEDY & VOLICH ARCHITECTURE

Portable Light pieces are created by women
weavers in the San Andreas region of the
Sierra Madre, Mexico, who are weaving the
portable light technology into textiles using
traditional back-strap looms and sewing
techniques. Portable Light combines high-
brightness LEDs from pedestrian walk signals, water-resistant tactile switches from
dishwashers, and rechargeable batteries
from the cell-phone industry, all sourced
from consumer appliances and standard
technologies. A portable, personalized
system, the units can be carried with their
owners to provide access to light and power
when needed. The Huichol shape the light
to their particular needs, using the textile
surfaces to provide direct, reflected, or
diffuse lighting, as needed for cottage-
based industries such as community
tortillerías, sandal making, repair work,
weaving, and beading.

SOLAR DISH KITCHEN

DESIGNER/MANUFACTURER: BaSIC Initiative
Mexico Program of the University of Texas
and the University of Washington
Mexico, 2004
Aluminum, steel
DIMENSIONS: 5′ radius (training),
15′ radius (standard)
USED IN: India, Mexico

COURTESY OF SERGIO PALLERONI AND BASIC INITIATIVE,
UNIVERSITY OF TEXAS

Solar Dish Kitchen was designed for two
informal poor urban settlements (squatter
communities) in Mexico. Cooking meals for
their children was one way the mothers

organized themselves to supplement the
diets of their children and reduce costs.
A retrofit to an existing school incorporates
solar cooking, solar hot-water heating,
grey-water filters to treat the dishwater,
natural light as the main source of lighting,
rainwater catchment, and photovoltaic
panels to allow the kitchen to go off the
grid. The Solar Dish is built from bicycle
parts, and small vanity mirrors create the
parabolic mirror surface which concentrates the energy of the sun on a pot or
stove in the kitchen. The community and
local government plan to build more
kitchens based on this prototype.

More than two billion people around the world (one-third of
the global population) have no access to grid electricity.

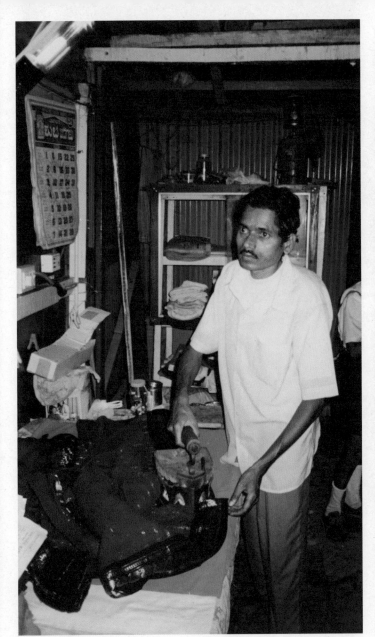

SOLAR HOME LIGHTING SYSTEM

DESIGNER/MANUFACTURER:

SELCO-India

India, 1994

Solar panel, luminaries, charge controller

DIMENSIONS: 1.5 h x 21 w x 26 d
(solar panel), 2 h x 6 w x 6 d (charge
controller), 14 h x 4 w x 14 d (luminaries)

USED IN: Bhutan, India, Sri Lanka, Vietnam

COURTESY OF SELCO-INDIA

Electricity reaches only a limited portion of the world's population. More than 1.6 billion people worldwide lack connection to an electrical network. Candles and kerosene and oil lamps are still some of the most common options for basic lighting, with dry cells and automotive batteries used to power radios, televisions, and small appliances. These sources are low-quality, cumbersome, expensive, and often dangerous, but they are the only available options to rural families, small farmers, businesses, and institutions. The Solar Home Lighting System, a wireless solar-power system originally designed for rural and peri-urban customers in India, enables families to improve their productivity by allowing them to pursue income-generating activities in the evening while their children have better light for studying.

SOLAR AID

DESIGNER/MANUFACTURER:

Godisa Technologies
Botswana, 2003
UV-resistant ABS plastic, 680-ohm resistor,
10-kilo-ohm resistor, 100-ohm resistor,
transistor, diode, LED, batteries, solar
panel, rubber, screws

DIMENSIONS: 4.5 h x 1 w x 3 d (charger)

USED IN: Angola, Bolivia, Botswana, Brazil,
Cambodia, Cameroon, Canada, Columbia,
Costa Rica, Democratic Republic of Congo,
Dominican Republic, Ethiopia, France,
Germany, Guatemala, Haiti, India, Israel,
Kenya, Madagascar, Malawi, Mexico,
Palestine, Paraguay, Philippines, South
Africa, Swaziland, Tanzania, Trinidad and
Tobago, United Kingdom, United States,
Vietnam, Yemen, Zambia, Zimbabwe

Approximately 10% of the world population
has a disabling hearing impairment, and
80% of them live in developing countries.
The most expensive part of a hearing aid is
the battery, which needs to be continually
replaced. The Solar Aid solar-powered
hearing-aid battery recharger, developed in
Botswana, helps those with hearing
disabilities afford to continue in school and
participate in economy activity. More than
7,000 units are in use in South America,
Central America, Africa, and Asia. And
because batteries are generally expensive
everywhere, Godisa Technologies intends
to make this affordable technology widely
available not just in developing countries
but also in the United States and Europe.

At least 1.3 billion people worldwide lack access to the
most basic healthcare.

STARSIGHT

DESIGNER: Kolam Partnership Ltd.

MANUFACTURER: nex-g Singapore Malaysia and Indonesia, 2007
Light, battery, nex-g WiFi receiver, solar panel

DIMENSIONS: Varies on location; U.S. version is 16.5′ high for residential areas; Vietnamese version is at least 19.7′ high

USED IN: Cameroon, Côte d'Ivoire, Republic of Congo

COURTESY OF LAURENT GBAGBO, PRESIDENT, CÔTE D'IVOIRE

The StarSight system combines solar-powered street lighting and Internet access in a wireless configuration, bypassing conventional power and telephone grids. StarSight provides a more secure environment, connectivity for building an emerging economy, and emergency communication and lighting for areas hit by disaster.

SUGARCANE CHARCOAL

DESIGNER/MANUFACTURER: MIT D-Lab
Haiti, 2004–05
Bagasse, cassava root binder,
55-gallon oil drum kiln, D-Lab press
DIMENSIONS: 3´ h x 2´ diameter (55-gallon
oil drum), 2´ h x 1´ w x 8 d (briquette press),
2´ h x 18 diameter (traditional stove)
USED IN: Haiti, Ghana; Brazil, India
(field demonstrations)

COURTESY OF AMY SMITH, MIT D-LAB

In Haiti, the production of wood charcoal,
the primary source of cooking fuel, contributes to severe deforestation and environmental degradation. More than 90% of

Haiti is now deforested. Many children die
of respiratory infections from breathing
indoor cooking fumes. Sugarcane charcoal
was developed as an alternative to wood
charcoal. Dried bagasse, the waste product
from sugarcane processing, is burned in
a simple kiln, carbonized, mixed with a
binder, and compacted using a press to produce sugarcane charcoal briquettes, which
burn as well as wood charcoal. Other agricultural waste materials such as corncobs
are being explored as other "food for fuel"
alternatives. Corncobs do not need further
processing after burning, eliminating the
need for binders and briquetting equipment
and significantly reducing the cost of charcoal production.

Wood-fuel consumption causes severe deforestation and fuel shortages in many areas of
the world, including Haiti, the Andean Highlands, the Sudan, Senegal, and Honduras.

SUPER MONEYMAKER PUMP

DESIGNERS: Robert Hyde, Martin Fisher,
Mark Butcher, Adblikadir Musa

MANUFACTURER: KickStart International
China, Kenya, and Tanzania, 1998
Mild steel, PVC, rubber

DIMENSIONS: 48 h x 14 w x 32 d

USED IN: Angola, Burkina Faso, Burundi,
Democratic Republic of Congo, Ethiopia,
Gambia, Ghana, Haiti, Kenya,
Madagascar, Malawi, Mali, Mozambique,
Nigeria, Philippines, Rwanda, Sierra
Leone, Somalia, South Africa, Sudan,
Tanzania, Uganda, Zambia, Yemen,
Zimbabwe,

COURTESY OF KICKSTART INTERNATIONAL

The Super MoneyMaker Pump is a manual treadle pump that will direct water to where it is needed, pulling water from a depth of seven meters and lifting it up fourteen meters above the water source. No fuel or electricity is required to operate the pump. The pump can irrigate a two-acre area over an eight-hour period. More than 50,000 Super MoneyMaker Pumps have been shipped to customers all over the world, and, based on KickStart's impact-monitoring studies, there are an estimated 35,000 households starting profitable small farm businesses using pumps to irrigate their fruits and vegetables during the dry season. By greatly increasing the yield, growing higher-value crops, and growing year round, these families have increased their net farm income from $110 to $1,100 per year—lifting themselves out of poverty.

WATER STORAGE SYSTEM

DESIGNER: International Development Enterprises (IDE) India
MANUFACTURER: Local workshops
India, 2006
Plastic
DIMENSIONS: 2′ h x 4′ w x 8′ d or smaller size, 500 liter or 1000 liter
USED IN: India

COURTESY OF PAUL POLAK, IDE

The low-cost, non-evaporative Water Storage System captures and stores monsoon rainwater, making water available for domestic and small plot micro-irrigation during India's long dry season. For many small farmers, there is either too much water during the rainy season or an acute water shortage during the dry season, when there not only is no water available for irrigation, but drinking-water wells run dry, requiring emergency drinking-water supplies. By providing a 10,000-liter plastic storage bag and enclosing it in a hand-dug pit, this system is one-fifth the cost of existing ferro-cement tanks.

WORLDBIKE PROTOTYPE

DESIGNER/MANUFACTURER: Paul Freedman,
Nate Byerley, Russ Rotondi, Jeremy Faludi,
with Gian Bongiorno and Dave Strain
(prototype fabrication assistance)
United States, Taiwan, China,
or India, 2003
Steel (Cro-Moly steel or high-tensile steel)
DIMENSIONS: 40 h x 22 w x 78 d
USED IN: Kenya (field test)

COURTESY OF WORLDBIKE

Worldbike exists as a challenge to the bicycle industry, particularly in the world's bicy-
cling centers of Taiwan, China, and India, to
design bicycles for customers in developing
countries. The bike weighs about the same
as the inexpensive single-speed bicycles
sold throughout East Africa, but is engi-
neered to be comfortable, safe, stylish, with
a higher carrying capacity.

The majority of road networks in developing countries primarily support bicycles
and horse-drawn carts rather than any form of motorized transportation.

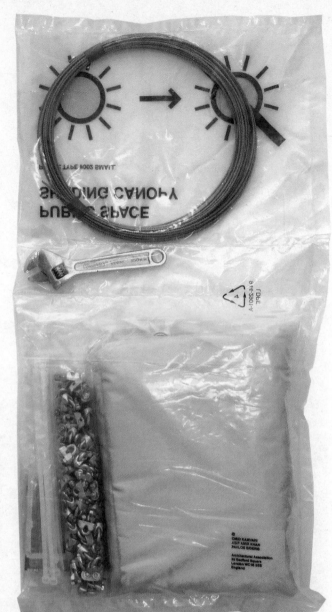

PUBLIC SPACE
SHADING CANOPY

RECIFE TYPE #002 SMALL

INCLUSIVE EDGE CANOPY

DESIGN/MANUFACTURING TEAM: Omid Kamvari, Asif Amir Khan, Pavlos Sideris (designers), Michael Hensel, Achim Menges (tutors), Architectural Association, London; André Moraes, Cynthia Pereira, Adryana Rozendo, Universidade Federal de Recife (project team); residents of Favela Do Pilar, Brazil Brazil, 2006
Lycra/Spandex, brass eyelets, steel cable, cable ties, cable grips, spanner
DIMENSIONS: varies upon location
USED IN: Brazil

COURTESY OF ASIF KHAN, OMID KAMVARI, AND PAULOS SIDERIS

The Inclusive Edge canopy creates public space for the favela community of Pilar in Recife, Brazil, by providing shade at a low cost. Material is stretched over the street and fixed to points on existing trees, roofs, water tanks, poles, and shop fronts with the help of local residents. More than mere shade results from the canopy, under which a flexible space emerges. Residents gather to find respite from the glaring heat of the sun, groups of children play in the shade, factory workers eat lunch, and neighbors gather to converse. The canopy and space underneath engender pride and a sense of community, and the identifiable yellow color of the canopy acts as a neighborhood landmark.

SELECTED STATISTICS: THE OTHER 90%

ANDREA LIPPS

- The world's total population is 6.5 billion. Ninety percent, or close to 5.8 billion people, lack the means to purchase even the most basic goods. (U.S. Census Bureau; UN Development Program; *Strategy + Business*)
- Almost half the world's population, or 2.8 billion people, live on less than $2 a day. One in six people around the world, or about 1.1 billion, exist on less than $1 a day. (World Bank)
- Two-thirds of those living in extreme poverty live in Asia. In sub-Saharan Africa, 350 million people, or half that region's population, live on less than the equivalent of $1 a day. (UNICEF)
- One billion children live in poverty worldwide, most of whom live in South Asia and sub-Saharan Africa. (UNICEF; UN Department of Social and Economic Affairs)
- Women are among the poorest of the world's poor, representing 70% of the 1.1 billion people who live in extreme poverty. (Office of the UN High Commissioner for Human Rights; UNIFEM)
- Of the approximately 1.1 billion people in the world living in extreme poverty, about 800 million live in rural regions. (International Fund for Agricultural Development)
- The combined wealth of the world's 200 richest individuals hit $1 trillion in 1999. By contrast, the combined income of the 582 million people living in the forty-three least developed countries was $146 billion. (UN Development Program)
- In 2005, 37 million people, 12.6% of the United States' total population, were living in poverty. (U.S. Census Bureau)

SHELTER

- More than one billion people worldwide live in inadequate housing, with more than 100 million people living in conditions classified as homeless. (Office of the UN High Commissioner for Human Rights)
- Six hundred forty million children in developing countries live without adequate housing. (UNICEF)
- There are currently 21 million internally displaced persons, in addition to 12 million refugees and asylum seekers, needing temporary shelter. (Médecins Sans Frontières/Doctors Without Borders)
- Hurricane Katrina left an estimated 1.5 million Americans homeless in the Gulf Coast region. (National Law Center on Homelessness and Poverty)
- In the United States, approximately 3.5 million people experience homelessness each year. (Urban Institute)

WATER AND SANITATION

- More than one billion people do not have access to safe drinking water. Nearly two billion people live without access to basic sanitation. (*American Journal of Tropical Medicine and Hygiene*)

- One in five children—nearly 400 million—have no access to safe water. (UNICEF)
- Each day, 3,900 children die because they lack access to safe drinking water and adequate sanitation. (UNICEF)
- Waterborne diseases are estimated to cause more than two million deaths annually.
(*American Journal of Tropical Medicine and Hygiene*)

FOOD

- More than 840 million people in the world are malnourished, of whom 799 million live in the developing world. (CARE)
- Every year, six million children under the age of five die as a result of hunger. (CARE)
- Over 150 million children are malnourished, 50% of whom live in South Asia. (UNICEF)
- Rates of malnutrition are generally 150% higher in rural areas than urban areas. (UNICEF)

ENERGY

- Seventy percent of people in the developing world have no access to electricity in their homes, health clinics, or schools. (Solar Electric Light Fund)
- For three billion people, the main source for domestic energy needs is biomass fuels—wood, animal dung, crop residues, and coal. (World Health Organization)
- Wood remains the most important source of energy for two billion people in developing countries, who have little access to other sources of energy. (Food and Agriculture Organization of the United Nations)
- Wood-fuel consumption causes severe deforestation and shortages of fuel in many areas of the world, including Haiti, the Andean highlands, the Sahelian countries, and large cities in the Sudan, Senegal, and Honduras. (World Energy Council)
- Compared with gas stoves, wood-burning stoves release fifty times more particulate matter, carbon monoxide, and hydrocarbons during cooking. (World Health Organization)
- It is estimated that 2.5 million deaths each year result from indoor exposure to particulate matter from burning biomass fuels. (World Health Organization)
- More than two billion people around the world have no access to grid electricity. (UN Environment Program)
- Nine out of ten Africans do not have access to electricity. (UN Environment Program)

HEALTH

- At least 1.3 billion people lack access to the most basic healthcare. (World Health Organization)
- One in seven children—270 million—have no access to health services. (UNICEF)
- Malaria slows economic growth in Africa by an estimated 1.3% a year. (World Bank)
- Approximately 90% of malaria deaths occur in sub-Saharan Africa, where one million people, most of them children under five, die each year from the disease. (World Bank)

EDUCATION

- Eight hundred fifty-five million people worldwide are illiterate. Of that number, two-thirds are women. (UNICEF)
- One hundred twenty-one million children worldwide, the majority of whom are girls, are not enrolled in primary school. (UNICEF)
- Less than 15% of the world's total population has Internet access. (Internet World Statistics)

TRANSPORT

- It is estimated that about 900 million rural dwellers in developing countries do not have reliable, all-season access to main road networks, and about 300 million do not have any form of motorized access. (World Bank)
- The majority of road networks in developing countries support bicycles and horse-drawn carts, rather than any form of motorized transportation. (World Bank)
- In rural Africa, women transport more than three times as many goods as men, often by carrying fuel, water, and produce on their heads, at great cost to their physical health. In sub-Saharan Africa, women often spend fifteen to thirty hours a week transporting water, firewood, crops, and grains for milling. (World Bank)

For additional statistics and information, please visit the Web sites of the organizations cited.

SELECTED REFERENCES

Architecture for Humanity, ed. *Design Like You Give a Damn: Architectural Responses to Humanitarian Crises.* New York: Metropolis Books, 2006.

Bornstein, David. *How to Change the World: Social Entrepreneurs and the Power of New Ideas.* Oxford: Oxford University Press, 2004.

Easterly, William. *The White Man's Burden: Why the West's Efforts to Aid the Rest Have Done So Much Ill and So Little Good.* New York: Penguin Press, 2006.

Farmer, Paul. *Pathologies of Power.* Berkeley: University of California Press, 2005.

Leonard, David K., and Scott Straus. *Africa's Stalled Development: International Causes and Cures.* Boulder, CO: Lynne Rienner, 2003.

Levine, Ruth, et al. *Millions Saved: Proven Successes in Global Health.* Washington, DC: Center for Global Development, 2004.

Papanek, Victor. *Design for the Real World: Human Ecology and Social Change.* Chicago: Academy Chicago Publishers, 1984.

Prahalad, C. K. *The Fortune at the Bottom of the Pyramid: Eradicating Poverty through Profits.* Upper Saddle River, NJ: Wharton School Publishing, 2005.

Sachs, Jeffrey D. *The End of Poverty: Economic Possibilities for Our Time.* New York: Penguin Books, 2005.

Schumacher, E. F. *Small is Beautiful: Economics as if People Mattered*, rev. ed. New York: Harper & Row Publishers, 1989.

Sen, Amartya. *Development as Freedom.* New York: Alfred A. Knopf, 1999.

Steffen, Alex, ed. *Worldchanging: A User's Guide for the 21st Century.* New York: Harry N. Abrams, 2006.

Wint, Guy, ed. *Asia: A Handbook.* London: Anthony Blond, 1966.

Yunus, Muhammed. *Banker to the Poor: Micro-Lending and the Battle against World Poverty.* New York: PublicAffairs, 1999.

SELECTED ORGANIZATIONS

For further information about many of the organizations included in *Design for the Other* 90%, please visit www.cooperhewitt.org as well as the following Web sites:

Advanced Micro Devices (AMD): 50x15.amd.com
American Assistance for Cambodia:
    www.cambodiaschools.com
Architectural Association, London: www.aaschool.ac.uk
BASIC Initiative: www.basicinitiative.org
Bhagwan Mahaveer Viklang Sahayata Samiti, Jaipur:
    www.jaipurfoot.org
CITYbuild Consortium of Schools: www.citybuild.org
Center for Connected Health (Partners Telemedicine):
    www.connected-health.org
Construction Management & Consulting Services
    (COMAC), Ltd.: www.comacltd.com
Continuum: www.dcontinuum.com
Design that Matters: www.designthatmatters.org
First Miles Solutions: www.firstmilesolutions.com
fuseproject: www.fuseproject.com
Global Village Shelters, LLC: www.gvshelters.com
Godisa Technologies: www.godisa.org
Green Project: www.thegreenproject.org
House of Dance & Feathers:
    www.houseofdanceandfeathers.org
International Development Enterprises (IDE): www.ide.org
Kennedy & Violich Architecture, Ltd.: www.kvarch.net
KickStart International: www.kickstart.org
LifeStraw: www.lifestraw.com
M3 Design: www.m3designinc.com
Mad Housers, Inc.: www.madhousers.org
Meridian Design, Inc.: www.uvaquastar.com
MIT D-Lab: http://web.mit.edu/d-lab/
One Laptop per Child: www.laptop.org
PermaNet: www.permanet.com
Portable Light Project: www.caup.umich.edu/portablelight
Potters for Peace: www.pottersforpeace.org
Project Locus: www.projectlocus.org
Public Architecture: www.publicarchitecture.org
Q Drum (Pty) Ltd.: www.qdrum.co.za
Ratanakiri: www.ratanakiri.com
SELCO-India: www.selco-india.com
Side by Side International: www.side-by-side-intl.org
Squid Labs: www.squid-labs.com
Star Sight: www.starsightproject.com
University of Kansas School of Architecture and Urban
    Planning: www.saud.ku.edu
WorldBike: www.worldbike.org
YouOrleans: www.artcenter.edu/designmatters

For further information about other organizations which offered information, insights, and support for the exhibition, please visit the following Web sites:

AIGA Aspen Design Summit: www.aiga.org
Architecture for Humanity:
    www.architectureforhumanity.org
CARE: www.care.org
Design Corps: www.designcorps.org
Doctors Without Borders:
    www.doctorswithoutborders.org
Industrial Designers of America: www.idsa.org
International Fund for Agricultural Development:
    www.ifad.org
National Endowment for the Arts: www.nea.org
National Law Center on Homelessness and Poverty:
    www.nlchp.org
New Orleans Wiki:
    www.thinknola.com/wiki/New_Orleans_Wiki
Office of the United Nations High Commissioner for
    Human Rights: www.unhchr.ch
Oxfam America: www.oxfamamerica.org
Rolex Awards for Enterprise: www.rolexawards.com
UNICEF: www.unicef.org
UNIFEM: www.unifem.org
United Nations: www.un.org
Urban Institute: www.urban.org
U.S. Census Bureau: www.census.gov
World Bank: www.worldbank.org
World Energy Council: www.worldenergy.org
World Health Organization: www.who.int
World Revolution: www.worldrevolution.org
World Wildlife Fund: www.worldwildlife.org

ACKNOWLEDGMENTS

Cynthia Smith and Cooper-Hewitt, National Design Museum would like to thank the following individuals and organizations, listed in no particular order, for their invaluable help and cooperation during the preparation of the *Design for the Other 90%* exhibition and book.

DESIGN FOR THE OTHER 90% ADVISORY BOARD

Bryan Bell, Founder and Executive Director, Design Corps

Cheryl Heller, CEO, Heller Communication Design

Martin J. Fisher, Ph.D., Cofounder and Executive Director, KickStart International

Sergio Palleroni, Founder, BaSiC Initiative, Visiting Professor, Center for Sustainable Architecture, University of Texas

Dr. Paul R. Polak, Founder and President, International Development Enterprises (IDE)

Cameron Sinclair, Cofounder and Executive Director, Architecture for Humanity

Amy B. Smith, Instructor, Massachusetts Institute of Technology, and Cofounder, International Development Initiative

At Cooper-Hewitt: Shamus Adams, Debbie Ahn, Tom Andersen, Bill Berry, Jill Bloomer, Annie Chambers, Perry C. Choe, Lucy Commoner, Jocelyn Crapo, Aaron Crayne, Melanie Fox, Diane Galt, Lauren Gray, Chris Jeannopoulos, Mei Mah, Matilda McQuaid, Laurie Olivieri, Mick O'Shea, Robert Paasch, Wendy Rogers, Larry Silver, Nancy Sul, Katie Vagnino, Mathew Weaver. Formerly of Cooper-Hewitt: Alexxa Gotthardt

Tsang Seymour Design: Laura Howell, Patrick Seymour

Studio Lindfors: Erik Jostock, Ostap Rudakevych

Front Studio: Yen Ha, Michi Yanagishita

Gilsanz Murray Steficek, LLP: Victoria Arbitrio, Ramon Gilsanz

M3 Design: Adam Lerner, Jeff Mulhausen

Meridian Design, Inc.: Kurt Kuhlmann, Dan Matthews

IDE: Deepak Adhikari, Kyle Boice, Linda Chang, Narayan Khawas, Aaron Langton, Michael Roberts, Kailash Sharma, Steve Wilson, Bob Yoder

WorldBike: Gian Bongiorno, Nate Byerly, Ross Evans, Jeremy Faludi, Paul Freedman, Adam French, Ed Lucero, Moses Odhiambo, Russ Rotondi, Matt Snyder, Dave Strain

Potters for Peace: Peter Chartrand, Ron Rivera

Centers for Disease Control: Daniele Lantagne

Porch Cultural Center: Ed Buckner, Helen Regis

Kennedy & Violich Architecture, Ltd.: Sheila Kennedy, Kyle Sturgeon

SELCO-India: H. Harish Hande

Godisa Technologies Trust: Modesta Nyirenda

Heller Communication Design: Devon Berger, Karina Hadida, Alexandra Pacheco, Gary Scheft

Public Architecture: John Cary, Liz Ogbu, John Peterson

COMAC Ltd.: Dr. Solomon Mwangi

KickStart International: Mark Butcher, Edward Chan-Lizardo, Robert Hyde, Michael Mills, Nick Moon, Adblikadir Musa, Martin Rogena, Ken Weimer

Global Village Shelters, LLC: Daniel Ferrara, Mia Yvonne Ferrara Pelosi II, Philip Suarez

House of Dance & Feathers: L. J. Goldstein, Ronald W. Lewis

Project Locus: Patrick Rhodes

Kansas State University: Caitlin Heckathorn

United Villages, Inc.: Amir Alexander Hasson

American Assistance for Cambodia: Meng Dy, Bernard Krisher, Nuon So Thero

Partners Telemedicine: Paul Heinzelmann, M.D.

Side by Side International: Akiko Matsumoto

Sihanouk Hospital Center of HOPE: Rithy Chau

Honda Motor Co., Ltd.: Takato Ito, Marina Nagai, Rich Tsukamoto

GCX Distributors: Ben Kiasrithanakorn

Shin Satellite: Piyanuch Sujpluem

Kyocera Corporation: Isao Yukawa, Yuji Sugiyama, Hidehito Hisa

Bhagwan Mahavir Viklang Sahayata Samiti: D. R. Mehta

Green Project: David Reynolds, Jonathan Wallick

Renewable and Appropriate Energy Laboratory, University of California: Daniel Kammen

Rural Technology Enterprises: Charles Gitundu, Evans Kituyi

AFREPREN/FWD: Stephen Karekezi, Waeni Kithyoma, Oscar Onguru

Design that Matters, Inc.: Timothy Prestero

Harvard University, Kennedy School of Government: Randi Purchia

Vestergaard Frandsen S.A.: Mikkel Vestergaard Frandsen, Torben Vestergaard Frandsen, Brian M Hollingsworth, Harprit Kaur, Allan Mortensen, Thomas D. Soerensen

Mad Housers: Salma Abdulrahman, Nick Hess, Susan Lee

Kolam Partnership: Asif Khan, Omid Kamvari, Pavlos Sideris

Architectural Association, London: Antonia Lloyd

Cascade Designs: Whitney Persch

One Laptop per Child: Nicholas Negroponte, Nia Lewis

fuseproject: Yves Béhar, Mark Elkin, Leslie Ann Ruiz

Continuum: Kerry Emberley, Kevin Young

Mohammed Bah Abba

The Rolex Awards for Enterprise

Q Drum (Pty) Ltd.: Hans Hendrikse, Pieter Hendrikse
University of Kansas, School of Architecture: Rob Corser,
    Dan Etheridge, Nils Gore Christopher Huchon
Oliver Rothschild
Yannick Gaillac
Art Center College of Design: Mariana Amatullo, Jae Chae,
    Erica Clark, John Emshwiller, Janet Ferrero, Nik
    Hafermaas, Paul Hauge, Ayumi Ito, Atley Kasky,
    Matthew Potter, Elisa Ruffino
Harvard Business School, Social Enterprise Initiative:
    Andrea E. McGrath
Design Corps: Bryan Bell
Architecture for Humanity: Kate Stohr
Oxfam America, Mississippi: Deborah Bey
AIGA: Dorothy Dunn
Aspen Design Summit
St. Bernard Parish Tourist Commission:
    Elizabeth McDougall
National Endowment for the Arts: Jeff Speck
Laura A. Berenson
Design for the Majority: Leslie Speer
Industrial Designers Society of America
University of Illinois: Robert L. Thompson
Medical Care Development International:
    Ronald Marrocco
CITYbuild Consortium of Schools: Sarah Gamble
Coastal Women for Change: Sharon Hanshaw

For more information on the Museum and
the exhibition, visit Cooper-Hewitt's Web site,
www.cooperhewitt.org.

PHOTOGRAPHIC CREDITS

We are grateful to the organizations and individuals listed below for their permission to reproduce images in this book. Every effort has been made to trace and contact the copyright holders of the images reproduced. Any errors or omissions shall be corrected in subsequent editions. Numbers refer to figure numbers unless otherwise stated.

COVER: © 2005 Vestergaard Frandsen
BACK COVER: © Stanford Richins
CONTENTS PAGE: © 2006 Ed Lucero

BLOEMINK: 2. © Architecture for Humanity. 3: © Bhagwan
    Mahavir Viklang Sahayata Samiti. 4: © 2005 Palle Peter
    Skov. 5: © 2004 M3 Design. 6: © United Villages, Inc. 7:
    © 2002-2005 Design that Matters, Inc.
SMITH, CYNTHIA: 1: © 2005 Salma Abdulrahman. 2: © 2005
    Vestergaard Frandsen. 3: © 2005 KickStart
    International. 4: © 2006 Art Center College of Design.
    5: © 2006 Nils Gore. 6: © 2006 Patrick Rhodes. 7: ©
    2002 International Development Enterprises (IDE). 8:
    © 2006 Ed Lucero
POLAK: 1–6: © , 2002, 2003, 2004
    International Development Enterprises (IDE)
SMITH, AMY: 1–4, 5: © 2005 Bill Dolan. 4, 6–8:
    © 2006 Amy Smith
FISHER: 1, 2, 5, 6: © Allison Jones Photography. 3, 4, 7, 8: ©
    2004, 2006 KickStart International
NEGROPONTE/BÉHAR: 1, 3–5: © 2006 Mark Serr. 2:
    © 2006 fuseproject
HANDE: 1–4: © 1999, 2001, 2006 SELCO-India
HENDRIKSE: 1–5: © 1993, 2006 P. J. Hendrikse
PALLERONI (INFORMAL COMMUNITY SOLAR KITCHENS):
    1–6: © 2002, 2004 BaSiC Initiative
HELLER: 1: © WWF-Canon/Williams Amirtharaj Christy. 2:
    © WWF-Canon/Folke WULF
KENNEDY: 1, 2, 5: © KVA MATX. 3: © Stanford Richins. 4:
    © Stacy Schaefer, University of California, Chico
PALLERONI (KATRINA FURNITURE PROJECT): 1–3, 5–7:
    © 2006 BaSiC Initiative. 4: Cynthia Smith, © 2006
    Smithsonian Institution
PETERSON: 1–5: © 2006 Elena Dorfman, Photographer;
    Mende Design, Image Design and Compositing; John
    Peterson, Art Direction. 6, 7: © 2006 Public Architecture
NYIRENDA-ZABULA: 1–3: Matt Flynn,
    © 2006 Smithsonian Institution
BAH ABBA: 1–6: © 2000 Tomas Bertelsen
P. 84: (left) © Aleia McCord; (right) © M3 Design
P. 85: © Meridian Design, Inc.
P. 86: © 2003 International Development Enterprises (IDE)
P. 87: © 2006 Ed Lucero
P. 88: © 2005 International Development Enterprises (IDE)
P. 89: (left) © 2001 Daniele Lantagne; (right) © IDE Nepal
P. 90: © 2006 Public Architecture
P. 91: © KickStart International

ENDNOTES

BLOEMINK

1. The 90% figure represents, as Paul Polak of IDE notes, the fact that designers traditionally design work for only the wealthiest 10% of consumers in the industrialized world. Accurately defining international poverty levels themselves is an almost impossible task and more of an open discussion than a science. Many use the World Bank's "international poverty line" metric defined as those living on less than $1 per day. However, others like Sanjay G. Reddy and Thomas W. Pogge argue that, while valid for certain areas of the developing world, this represents an "arbitrary international poverty line that is not adequately anchored in any specification of the real requirements of human beings," and greatly understates the extent of global income poverty ("Monitoring Global Poverty: Better Options for the Future" paper dated November 18, 2002, the Carnegie Council on Ethics and International Affairs; and "How Not to Count the Poor," abstract from paper by Reddy and Pogge from October 29, 2005, ww.socialanalysis.org). Instead, Reddy and Pogge suggest a "human-requirements-centered" approach based on purchasing power parities.

SMITH, CYNTHIA

1. PovertyNet, "Overview: Understanding Poverty." World Bank, http://web.worldbank.org/WBSITE/EX-TERNAL/TOPICS/EXTPOVERTY/EXTPA/0,,contentMDK:2 0153855~menuPK:435040~pagePK:148956~piPK:216618~ theSitePK:430367,00.html (accessed 9/29/06).

2. Dashka Slater, "Earth's Innovators: Some people think outside the box. Some don't think about boxes at all." Massachusetts Institute of Technology International Development, http://web.mit.edu/idi/press/sierra-earth-innovators.pdf (accessed 9/29/06).

3. International Initiatives, "DesignMatters," Art Center College of Design, http://www.artcenter.edu/accd/international/int_ini-tiatives.jsp (accessed 9/30/06).

4. CITYbuild, "Mission Statement," http://www.city-build.org/mission.html (accessed 9/30/06).

5. "Hauser Center to be based at the Kennedy School of Government," in *The Harvard University Gazette* (April 17, 1997). Harvard University, http://www.hno.harvard.edu/gazette/1997/04.17/Multi disciplina.html (accessed 9/30/06).

6. Office of Engineering and Public Service, "2006–07 Engineering Service-Learning Courses." Stanford University, http://soe.stanford.edu /publicservice/courses0607.php (accessed 9/30/06).

7. The Design & Innovation Research Group, "Art & Design Research Centre." The University of Salford, http://www.adelphi.salford.ac.uk/adrc/dirg.html (accessed 9/30/06).

8. Leslie Speer, "The Next Decade of Design: Paradigm Shift," in *Innovation* 25 (2006): 31–35.

9. Pressroom, "10 Key Recommendations." United Nations Millennium Project, http://www.unmillenniumproject.org/press/press4.htm (accessed 9/29/06).

10. William Easterly, "UN 'fantasies' won't feed poor," letter to the *National Post*, February 25, 2006. New York University Development Research Institute, http://www.nyu.edu/fas/institute/dri/Easterly/File/UN%20fantasies%20own't%20feed%20poor.pdf#search=%22william%20easterly%20bottom-up%20searching%22 (accessed 9/29/06).

11. E. F. Schumacher, *Small is Beautiful, Economics as if People Mattered* (New York: Harper & Row Publishers, 1989), pp. 56–66.

12. Victor Papanek, *Design for the Real World: Human Ecology and Social Change* (Chicago: Academy Chicago Publishers, 1985).

13. PovertyNet, "Choosing and Estimating a Poverty Line." World Bank, http://web.worldbank.org/WBSITE/EXTERNAL/TOPICS/EXTPOVERTY/EXTPA/0,,contentMDK:20242879~menuPK:492130~pagePK:148956~piPK:216618~theSitePK:430367,00.html (accessed 9/29/06).

POLAK

1. Ernst Friedrich Schumacher, *Small Is Beautiful: Economics as if People Mattered* (London: Blond & Briggs Ltd., 1973).

SMITH, AMY

1. Bruce, N., R. Perez-Padilla, and R. Albalak, *The Health Effects of Indoor Air Pollution Exposure in Developing Countries* (Geneva: World Health Organization, 2002).

2. Bailis, R., M. Ezatti, and D. Kammen, "Mortality and Greenhouse Impacts of Biomass and Petroleum Energy Futures in Africa," in *Science*, vol. 308, April 2005.

3. WEC Survey for World Energy Resources, 2001.

4. I'd like to acknowledge the work done on this project by the original charcoal group: Shawn Frayne, Jamy Drouillard, Tilke Judd and Anna Bautista, Rachana Oza, Arthur Musah, and Andrew Levin; our initial community partners: Gerthy Lahens, Joazar Lucien and Nothude Tilus; and the second wave of charcoal researchers: Amy Banzaert, Jessica Vechakul, Andrew Heafitz, Victoria Fan, Alia Whitney-Johnson, and Jules Walter.

KENNEDY

1. For further thinking on this topic, see Sheila Kennedy, *Material Mis-Use* (London: The Architectural Association, 2000).

2. In current Portable Light prototypes, a solar charge time of two and a half hours provides nine hours of light bright enough to read by (45 lumens), or double that brightness (90 lumens) for four hours of task lighting.

3. Diaz Romo, Patricia; *Huicholes y Plaguacitas* (New York: Latin American Video Archives, 1993).

4. Carlson, Laura; International Relations Center, 1996,

http://www.irc-online.org/content/inside/93. The Solar Electric Light Fund has documented a direct correlation between the ability to use light at home and adult literacy. Without access to light, children and women who work during the day cannot study after sundown. Wood and kerosene sources pose serious health problems and are insufficient light sources for reading, proving only two to four useful lumens of light, compared with a single one-watt LED (40–90 lumens or more) or a 60-watt incandescent light bulb (900 lumens); see www.self.org.

5. Findings presented to the author in correspondence in May 2005 by Susanna Valadez, Cofounder and Director of the NGO Centro Huichol, in Huejuquilla, Jalisco State.

6. I am grateful for the help of Miguel Carrillio, Huichol Community Leader, Susanna Valadez, Dr. Carmen Huerta, and Stacy Schaefer in coordinating these efforts in the Sierra. I would like to thank my graduate students in the 2005 Nomads & Nanomaterials research studio for their work in helping to develop the applications and textile prototypes created by the Portable Light Team in 2004. For more information on this work, see www.portablelight.tcaup.edu.

7. See Zingg, Robert M., *Huichol Mythology* (Tucson: University of Arizona Press, 2004), on myths of the dry-season cycle.

8. For information on an extensive body of work documenting the role of the traditional weaving process in Huichol communities, see Schaefer, Stacy B., *To Think with a Good Heart* (Salt Lake City: University of Utah Press, 2002).

9. Anthropologists Peter Jimenez and Stacy Schaefer have pointed to the problems of how infrastructure can create forms of economic dependency, as has occurred in areas of San Andreas, where the government has installed the electrical grid as a way to encourage tourism in indigenous areas.

10. For arguments that development requires the removal of major sources of "unfreedoms," such as neglect of public facilities, poor economic opportunities, and systemic social deprivation, see Sen, Amartya, *Development as Freedom* (New York: Alfred A. Knopf, 1999), and Farmer, Paul, *Pathologies of Power* (Berkeley: University of California Press, 2005).

PALLERONI (KATRINA FURNITURE PROJECT)

1. From "Science and Human Needs," by Bruce Alberts, President of the National Academy of Sciences, given at its 137th annual meeting.

DESIGN FOR THE OTHER 90%

Design for the Other 90%
Copyright © 2007 Smithsonian Institution

Published by
Cooper-Hewitt, National Design Museum
Smithsonian Institution
2 East 91st Street
New York, NY 10128, USA
www.cooperhewitt.org

Published on the occasion of the exhibition
Design for the Other 90%
at Cooper-Hewitt, National Design Museum,
Smithsonian Institution,
May 4–September 23, 2007.

Distributed to the trade worldwide by
Assouline Publishing
601 West 26th Street, 18th floor
New York, NY 10001, USA
www.assouline.com

Design for the Other 90% is made possible by The Lemelson
Foundation. Additional funding is provided by public funds
from the New York State Council on the Arts, a State
agency, the Esme Usdan Exhibition Endowment Fund, and
the Ehrenkranz Fund.

This publication is made possible in part by
The Andrew W. Mellon Foundation.

First edition: May 2007
ISBN: 0-910503-97-4

Library of Congress CIP data available
from the publisher.

Museum Editor: Chul R. Kim, Head of Publications
Design: Tsang Seymour Design, Inc.
Printed in China on 100% recycled paper by Oceanic
Graphic Printing.